D0250985

A LIFETIME
OF RICHES

Michael J. Ritt, Jr. and Kirk Landers

A LIFETIME OF RICHES

THE BIOGRAPHY OF
NAPOLEON HILL

A DUTTON BOOK

DUTTON
Published by the Penguin Group
Penguin Books USA Inc., 375 Hudson Street,
New York, New York 10014, U.S.A.
Penguin Books Ltd, 27 Wrights Lane,
London W8 5TZ, England
Penguin Books Australia Ltd, Ringwood,
Victoria, Australia
Penguin Books Canada Ltd, 10 Alcorn Avenue,
Toronto, Ontario, Canada M4V 3B2
Penguin Books (N.Z.) Ltd, 182–190 Wairau Road,
Auckland 10, New Zealand

Penguin Books Ltd, Registered Offices:
Harmondsworth, Middlesex, England

First published by Dutton, an imprint of Dutton Signet,
a division of Penguin Books USA Inc.
Distributed in Canada by McClelland & Stewart Inc.

First Printing, July, 1995
10   9   8   7   6   5   4   3   2

 REGISTERED TRADEMARK—MARCA REGISTRADA

LIBRARY OF CONGRESS CATALOGING-IN-PUBLICATION DATA:

Landers, Kirk.
A lifetime of riches : a biography of Napoleon Hill / Kirk Landers and Michael J. Ritt, Jr.
p.   cm.
Includes index.
ISBN 0-525-94146-0
1. Hill, Napoleon, 1883-1970.   2. Businessmen—United States—Biography.   3. Success
in business—United States.   I. Ritt, Michael J.   II. Title.
HC102.5.H538L36   1995
158'.1'092—dc20

[B]   94-48789
                                                                                CIP

Printed in the United States of America
Set in Bembo and Spire
Designed by Julian Hamer

This book is printed on acid-free paper. ∞

CONTENTS

FOREWORD

It was my good fortune to be the first employee of the Napoleon Hill Associates. When Dr. Hill and W. Clement Stone formed Napoleon Hill Associates in 1952 to publish and distribute the Positive Mental Attitude (PMA) philosophy of success, I was working for Mr. Stone, managing the audiovisual services department of Combined Insurance Company of America. They asked me to record their lectures and to help with seminars and training programs they planned to offer.

For ten years, I traveled the country with these incredible men, recording their lectures, helping in the training sessions, and developing the promotional and teaching materials that they used. It was an experience afforded to very few, one that I shall always cherish. I can imagine nothing finer than to be able to work with such extraordinary people to help positively influence the lives of millions of people around the world.

When the Napoleon Hill Foundation was organized to serve as a vehicle to collect Dr. Hill's works and spread his philosophy of personal achievement, his wife, Annie Lou, asked me to serve on the board of directors. It was my privilege to serve as the organization's executive director, a position that I continue to hold today.

Over the years, we've republished a number of Dr. Hill's books and we have published totally new works based on his lectures, seminars, training guides, and other archival material. All have been enthusiastically received by the thousands upon thousands of loyal followers who have seen their lives change for the better when they understood and applied the principles of success Dr. Hill spent his lifetime developing and writing about.

He was an inspirational speaker who motivated millions of people to take charge of their own lives, to create for themselves the future that they desired. Although I heard him speak countless times as we traversed the country spreading his message, I never failed to learn something new—and to be inspired—every time he spoke.

Assembling the information for this biography provided me with the opportunity to relive many of those grand moments and to rededicate myself to the perpetuation of the philosophy developed by this unique individual. It also allowed me to spend some time with Dr. Hill's son, David, who was enormously helpful in ensuring the historical accuracy of this work.

Napoleon Hill was and is an American treasure. He was a confidant of presidents and statesmen. The prominent men of several generations freely revealed their secrets of success to him. But he never forgot his humble origins. He considered it his sacred obligation to share with the world the knowledge about personal achievement that he had accumulated during his rich and varied life.

I shall be eternally grateful that I was privileged to know well this great man, and I hope that through the pages of this biography, you too can come to know the man who helped millions of ordinary people discover the greatness within themselves.

Michael J. Ritt, Jr.

INTRODUCTION

I had experienced firsthand the power of Napoleon Hill's ideas long before I met the man himself. It was 1937 and although I had been in business for fifteen years, I—like most other American businessmen—was struggling to recover from the Great Depression. Then something happened that changed my life forever.

I remember it as clearly today as if it were yesterday. Morris Pickus, a well-known sales executive and sales counselor, had called upon me trying to sell me on a book that he was promoting to sales organizations. I didn't like the book and didn't buy, but as he was leaving, Mr. Pickus gave me a copy of another book by a little-known author named Napoleon Hill. The book was titled *Think and Grow Rich!*

Hill's message was electrifying! As I turned the pages of this great book, I realized that I held in my hand the collective wisdom of the great achievers of the day. The principles that they used to achieve success were available to anyone. They could be adopted and applied by any individual who would take the time to study and understand them.

When I read *Think and Grow Rich!*, I realized that Hill's

philosophy absolutely coincided with my own. His was a message of hope supported by proven, actionable principles. He knew that what the mind could conceive and believe, the mind could achieve when the principles were tenaciously applied by those who have a Positive Mental Attitude.

I was particularly interested in what Hill called the Master Mind Alliance—two or more people working together in perfect harmony toward the achievement of a common objective. I realized that through the application of this principle I could leverage myself by aligning my interests with those of others. They could help me with the work I had been doing, freeing me for other activities.

I began by sending a copy of *Think and Grow Rich!* to each of my sales representatives. The results were instantaneous and awesome. Those who were willing to recognize, relate, assimilate, and apply the principles were inspired by the book's contents and became highly motivated to achieve personal and financial success.

My sales managers became builders of miracle salespeople. Their sales results were phenomenal. They achieved what those unfamiliar with the art of motivation believed was simply impossible. They accomplished astounding sales records, then promptly broke those records. I knew at the time that Napoleon Hill was destined for greatness.

Big things began to happen for me as a result of the success my sales representatives achieved. I went from struggling for simple survival to building an organization that numbered more than a thousand salespersons. My bills were paid, my investments and assets were increasing, and I bought a vacation home in Florida. I realized that the only limitations I would ever have would be those that I placed upon myself.

It was fifteen years before I met the author whose work changed my life, and it occurred in a totally unexpected way. I had been asked to speak at a meeting of the suburban Chicago North Shore Kiwanis Club. What I didn't know when I cheerfully accepted that invitation was that Napoleon Hill would be at the same meeting.

In truth, I didn't even know where Dr. Hill lived or if he was still around. I discovered that at age sixty-nine, he was very much alive and contributing, although he had slowed down a good deal in his later years. We very quickly discovered that our philosophies were still as compatible as they were when I first sent a copy of his book to my sales representatives.

Before the luncheon was over, I asked Dr. Hill to come out of retirement to continue to spread his powerful message of personal achievement. Despite the sacrifices he knew he would be required to make, he didn't hesitate. He said, "I will if you will be my general manager." Another trait we share is that we are both men of action. Before the luncheon was over, we had made a deal.

During the decade we worked together, we had the opportunity to speak to thousands and thousands of people about the principles of personal achievement. I know that we successfully motivated many of them to realize their potential to achieve any goal that they set for themselves as long as it doesn't violate the laws of God or the rights of their fellow men. I know this to be true because more than three decades later I still hear from them how this philosophy changed their lives for the better.

It has been my honor to serve as president of the Napoleon Hill Foundation and to play an active role in the perpetuation of this wonderfully practical philosophy of personal achievement. I shall always be indebted to Napoleon Hill for the profound influence he has had upon my life.

Dr. Hill passed away in 1970 at the age of eighty-seven, but his ideas will never die. They are as powerful today as they were when he first introduced them so many years ago. One of the great joys of my life has been watching each new generation discover for itself the great truths contained in Hill's writings. His is a philosophy that is destined to endure.

It can be said about Napoleon Hill that he achieved one of the world's noblest distinctions. He made our world a better world for this and future generations as a result of his having been a part of it. I know you will enjoy the story of his life, and I'm equally confident that you will receive an enormous benefit from the principles of success that he wrote about . . . if you will only apply them in your own life.

I wish you great success!

W. Clement Stone

CHAPTER 1

1883-1895

Napoleon Hill struggled into a turbulent, changing world on October 26, 1883, the firstborn child of Sara and James Hill of Wise County, Virginia.

It was a strange and difficult time to begin a life. In the West, the United States was playing out the last acts of her manifest destiny. Indian fighter George Armstrong Custer was just seven years dead. His conqueror, Sitting Bull, had even more recently been exiled to a reservation. Geronimo and other Apache chiefs were still fighting to maintain their freedom in the American Southwest, their hit-and-run guerrilla tactics extending the Indian wars for a few more years.

But even as America was solidifying her western expansion, the nation's focus was returning east, where power had passed from old money and landed gentry to a new generation of capitalist tycoons bent on carving empires for themselves in manufacturing and commerce.

By the time of Napoleon Hill's birth, America's factories and sweatshops were roiling with labor tensions that would reach a violent climax in the Haymarket Square riot of 1886, the first of many such violent confrontations that would take place during Hill's life. But the 1880s and 1890s were also a period when the American Dream would blossom brighter and more visibly than ever before, inspired by a steady procession of common men rising to positions of power and wealth. Among the most famous was Thomas Edison, whose stature and wealth as an inventor was firmly established by the time Hill was born. Indeed, just a few months before Hill's birth, Edison's lightbulbs illuminated a field in Fort Wayne, Indiana, for the playing of America's first night baseball game.

Another famous example was Andrew Carnegie, a self-made millionaire immigrant who had gambled his hard-fought wealth on an infant company in fledgling industry in 1873. When Hill was born ten years later, the Carnegie Steel Company had already emerged as one of the world's premier steel producers, and Andrew Carnegie was well on his way to converting mere wealth into one of the most colossal fortunes ever amassed by an individual.

Like millions of other Americans born into modest or impoverished means, Hill was destined to admire the likes of Edison, Carnegie, Henry Ford, and dozens of other self-made men with a passion that bordered on worship. Like millions of other Americans, he would become consumed with interest about people who succeed where others fail . . . why . . . and how to structure his own life to take a place among the rich and powerful. Like millions of Americans, he would dream of meeting these giants, impressing them, and harvesting the wisdom that produced their incredible accomplishments.

But unlike most of those other millions of admirers and wonderers, Napoleon Hill was destined to fulfill his dreams. He would not only meet and impress America's greatest achievers—dozens of them—he would also spend his entire adult life eliciting their secrets to success and communicating them to the world.

* * *

Wise County was a forgotten backwater region on the Kentucky border in the Blue Ridge Mountains. It was almost completely isolated from the frenetic changes taking place in America's cities and towns. To reach it from the outside world, one had to navigate more than one hundred miles through thick forests, deep valleys and gorges, and remote hollows. The roads ranged from rutted dirt tracks to rock-bottomed creek beds that could only be used between rains.

Life was primitive by the standards of Eastern city-dwellers. One- and two-room log cabins were the typical dwellings of the Wise County populace in the 1880s, and some lived in shelters simply carved out of the fallen trunks of huge trees. Life expectancies were short, infant mortality high, and tens of thousands of rural Virginians suffered from chronic health problems ranging from hookworm to malaria to pellagra, a disease caused by inadequate diet.

Except in a few major towns, public schools were in wretched shape throughout the state. Elementary schools were open for only about four months of the year, and attendance was not required. High schools were rare—numbering fewer than one hundred in the entire state—and most offered only a two- or three-year curriculum. Indeed, even twenty years after Hill's birth there were just 10 four-year high schools in all of Virginia.

Barter was more common than cash in Wise County and there were few well-to-do families. Many heated their homes by burning coal, lumps of which lay on the ground for the taking; commercial coal mining did not begin until the end of the decade and would finally come to southeast Virginia in the 1890s. Most made a living by combining farming with a trade and hunting for fresh meat. The thin, rocky soil and the rugged contours of the land made farming difficult in the best of times. But the 1880s were not the best of times in American agriculture. Depressed crop prices were driving a steady stream of families out of farming and into the cities in desperate search of a living wage.

In Wise County and the rest of Appalachia, those who stayed often survived by converting their meager corn crops into something more valuable—moonshine. And although they most often lived in close-knit cooperation with one another, violent feuds and quarrels could spark suddenly and last for years. Indeed, just two or three days' ride from Wise County, the most infamous mountain feud of all—between the Hatfields and the McCoys—started shortly before Napoleon's birth and would glow and flare for nearly two decades.

No wonder then that Napoleon Hill would later describe his birthplace as a two-room log cabin in a mountain culture famous for three things: feuds, moonshine, and ignorant people.

"For three generations my people had been born, lived, struggled in ignorance, illiteracy and poverty, and died without having been outside the mountains of that section," wrote Hill in his unpublished autobiography. "They made their living from the soil. Whatever money they procured was from the sale of corn converted into moonshine. . . . There were no railroads, telephones, electric lights or passable public highways."

Hill alluded often to his early childhood in his articles, books, and speeches. His recollections of those early years— shallow and entirely negative—helped lend dramatic proportions to his self-told rags-to-riches story. In another way, they reflected the feelings of a man who, even as a child, stood somewhat outside the circle of mountain culture.

James Monroe Hill, Napoleon's father, was neither ignorant nor illiterate, and it is unlikely he engaged in moonshining. He was one of six children of James Madison Hill, an English-born printer who immigrated to America in the

1840s with two brothers and settled in the Black Mountain area on the Kentucky-Virginia border.

James Monroe Hill took to mountain living in a way Napoleon never would. Like his neighbors, James Hill combined farming with other trades and services in demand in their isolated community. As a boy, he learned the printing trade from his father—as well as hunting and fishing and nature lore. He received a brief, crude public school education in a one-room log schoolhouse. At age fourteen his formal education was complete, and he began working in his father's printing business.

By the time he was seventeen years old, James had married Sara Sylvania Blair and built a cabin in a remote area on Guests River that later became a hamlet called Lipps. That year, he made his own printing press using a salvaged font of old type and a wooden press and chase he carved and chiseled from local timber. James used the press to publish the *Zephyr*, Wise County's first newspaper. It contained personals, local news, a brief mention about the weather, and a short editorial. In addition to printing and writing the copy, the young entrepreneur personally delivered the publication by horseback to its one hundred or so subscribers.

Publishing the *Zephyr* was a labor of love for James Hill— it produced little income and required a great deal of time. Thus, three years later when his first son was born, he suspended publication to put all his energies into providing for his young family. He had no difficulty finding other, more marketable pursuits for his talents. When Napoleon was born, James was a blacksmith and farmer; later, he put Lipps on the map by helping to establish a post office there, and he served as postmaster for many years. He was also a trader and merchant and ran a small general store. He did all these things well. In the mountain tradition, he was largely self-taught, substituting creativity and cleverness for formal training. His inspiration was the need to find solutions to his own and his neighbors' problems.

Sara and James named their first son Oliver Napoleon, the middle name coming from an uncle of James's who had immigrated with his father from England and, according to family accounts, made a success of himself. Perhaps in the hope that their eldest son would also make good, the family called him "Napoleon," and he eventually dropped "Oliver" from his name altogether.

Napoleon's earliest years marked him for anything but success, however. He was a wild, perhaps hyperactive child known to neighbors and family members mainly for the mischief he caused. One of his favorite pastimes was rolling rocks down a hill. On one particular day, a large rock he pitched dislodged a boulder that smashed through several fences and very nearly struck a neighbor's house before rolling to a stop nearby.

By Hill's own account, his parents started him in school at age four "mainly to get me off their hands while they worked in the fields."

Part of Napoleon's wildness may have stemmed from his mother's frail health. Little is known about Sara Hill, save that she bore Napoleon and his brother Vivian prior to dying when Napoleon was nine years old. By then, Napoleon considered himself the toughest boy in the county and posed a serious disciplinary problem for his father.

Stunned and lonely after his mother's death, Napoleon's penchant for pranks and mischief took a more foreboding direction. In a region where it was common even for young boys to hunt with rifles, Napoleon found a way to get everyone's attention. He began toting a real pistol—a six-shooter—and imagined himself in the role of his hero, Jesse James. A year later, when his father remarried, Napoleon's growing marksmanship and wildness had made him the terror of Guests River—and the subject of endless consternation to both James Hill and other members of the Hill clan who had tried fruitlessly to turn the boy around.

The Hill family's concern about young Napoleon's direction in life was well founded. While most of the people who settled in the Virginia-Kentucky border area in the 1880s and 1890s were industrious, resourceful, God-fearing families, the remote mountain wilderness had more than its share of lawless thugs who rode the backwoods trails packing pistols and knives that were used for robbery and murder. If young Napoleon were to reach adolescence still wanting to be an outlaw, he could find role models—and opportunities—almost literally in his own backyard.

Just as Napoleon's reputation for trouble was reaching its peak, a remarkable woman entered his life. A year after Sara's death, James Hill married Martha Ramey Banner, the widow of a school principal and daughter of a Coburn, Virginia, physician.

Nothing in her cultured upbringing prepared her for mountain living. But nothing, not even a pistol-toting ten-year-old stepson, could defeat her. A well-educated, dynamic woman, Martha saw in James Hill a kind, decent man with a raw genius for tinkering and inventing things. In her eldest stepson, the scourge of the county, she saw a restless, angry boy drifting toward self-destruction. In the Hill homestead, she saw poverty and a lack of direction that threatened the Hill children with a lifetime of ignorance, back-breaking labor, and failure. A lesser woman would almost certainly have waited for a less challenging situation, but Martha stepped in decisively. Soon after the marriage, Martha Hill gathered her three children and the Hills together and announced that she intended to change the mental, spiritual, and financial status of the entire family.

Several things happened very quickly after that. James Hill established the Lipps post office and began selling general merchandise. At Martha's insistence, the entire family became active in the Three Forks of Powell River Primitive Baptist Church. And Martha Hill made Napoleon her pet project.

The church undoubtedly helped Martha curb Napoleon's antisocial behavior; it not only provided religious training and worship but was also a primary thread in the area's social fabric. After several fiery sermons, the congregation would "open its doors" to hear and rule on charges of misconduct raised by one member against another. Penalties for the unrepentant could include banishment from the church and its social activities, as well as being shunned by church members outside the church. Though there is no record of it, Napoleon almost certainly was the focus of some of the open-door sessions; to avoid humiliation for himself and his family, he would have had to acknowledge his trespasses and pledge to do better in the future.

But Martha's work with Napoleon went far beyond the church and social pressure. She patiently constructed a close, individual relationship with her troubled stepson. She didn't force the stubborn, hot-tempered boy to do things, for this would most certainly have produced failure. Instead, she treated him like the person she wanted him to become— an intelligent, hard-working, independent lad who would set constructive goals for himself and achieve them. Her patience and respect paid off. When Napoleon was eleven years old, Martha called him into the living room for a private conversation.

"People are wrong about you, Napoleon," she said. "You're not the worst boy in the county, only the most active. You just need to direct your energy toward accomplishing something worthwhile." In the course of this conversation, Martha suggested that Napoleon consider becoming a writer because of his keen imagination and gutsy initiative. "If you will devote as much time to reading and writing as you have to causing trouble," she concluded, "you might live to see the time when your influence will be felt throughout the state."

Martha's vision was a revelation to young Napoleon. It was the first time anyone other than James or Sara had seen something good in him, and it was the first time he had ever considered winning fame beyond the borders of rural Wise County. Though he continued to practice with his six-shooter, he also attacked his education with unprecedented vigor, even at home, where Martha provided instruction far surpassing the rudimentary lessons available at school.

Like so many things in Napoleon's life, education did not come easily to him. Discipline and concentration were brutally difficult barriers, but with Martha's help he struggled gamely against his own nature and gradually began to succeed.

By the time Napoleon was twelve years old, Martha could see he was ready for the next step. Pulling him aside once more for a private talk, she proposed that if he would give up his six-gun, she would replace it with a typewriter—a rare and expensive device in 1895. "If you become as good with a typewriter as you are with that gun," said Martha, "you may become rich and famous and known throughout the world."

Napoleon was powerless to resist this temptation. Even at age twelve, he lusted for fame and fortune. His diligent reading had acquainted him with great books and great writers—and he had learned that writers can achieve fame that spreads beyond mere county, state, or national boundaries and even beyond one's own lifetime. Now, in one sweeping proposal, Martha gave Napoleon the chance to picture himself in that image.

Later in life, Napoleon Hill would popularize the phrase, "what the mind of man can conceive, it can achieve." And so it was with young Napoleon. The seed of a concept carefully planted and patiently nurtured by his stepmother began to take root and grow.

Without hesitation, Napoleon surrendered his pistol to Martha and agreed to her proposal. As he did so, his life as an unruly backwoods tough came to an end with utter finality and he cracked open the first door to his future—a future that lay far from the Blue Ridge Mountains, moonshine, and the struggle to scratch out a living from the soil.

Probably no one was more surprised than James Hill at the transformation that occurred in his adolescent son. Though he had watched with amazement for several years at the magic Martha worked on Napoleon, nothing prepared him for the sight of his once-feared son waiting with ecstatic anticipation for the arrival of his new typewriter—a weapon with which he would make the printed word far mightier than the sword.

CHAPTER 2

1895–1908

Nostalgic scribes would name it the Gay Nineties, the decade in which Napoleon Hill became aware of a world outside the mountains and valleys of Appalachia and Wise County. But it was more a decade of growing pains than gaiety for America. Like Napoleon, the country was lurching toward majority in uncoordinated spurts, different parts of her anatomy growing at different rates. Like an adolescent, she was fueled with boundless energy and enthusiasm to compensate for a lack of experience. Thus, through the 1890s and the early years of the twentieth century, America careened breathlessly forward from one unrecognized economic, social, and political barrier to the next, dodging and leaping a few, crashing violently into many.

Inevitably, the country's soaring leaps forward and devastating tumbles sent vibrations through a wide cross section of its citizenry, shaping lives and reshaping careers. Few people would be more dramatically affected by these volatile times than young Napoleon, for each sprint and stumble brought him ever closer to his unique destiny.

Even as the Hill family waited for Napoleon's typewriter

and the birth of a new son, Paul, in 1895, America was recovering from the Panic of 1893, one of many economic disasters of the late nineteenth century. This one involved a sudden loss of confidence in U.S. securities on the part of foreign investors following the failure of the Philadelphia and Reading Railroad and the National Cordage Company. As hordes of foreign investors sold their U.S. securities at fire-sale prices, tens of millions of dollars of investment capital disappeared from the American economy. Prices for corn, iron, cotton, and other commodities plunged. Farm foreclosures soared. One after another, the monopolistic trusts formed to control commodity prices collapsed into bankruptcy. Railroads slipped into receivership. Heavy industry stagnated, creating massive unemployment. More than six hundred banks and fifteen thousand institutions failed within a year, with the most grievous damage occurring in the South and West.

The residents of Wise County were no longer completely impervious to such havoc in the outside world. As corn prices evaporated to thirty-six cents a bushel, moonshining became a final alternative to failure and homelessness for many. In addition, the ensuing depression ravaged the growth of fledgling commercial coal-mining operations in the region, dashing the hopes of many who, like Martha Hill, wanted to change the financial and cultural status of their mountain families.

But the Hills' hopes and dreams continued to glow. Like Henry Ford, who completed his first gasoline engine shortly before the Panic of 1893 and spent the depression years working on a car that would be completed in 1896, the Hills pressed on.

Napoleon's utter fascination with the typewriter carried him through the torturous process of learning how to use it. The neat, clean lines and words lent order and formality to his

thoughts and ideas, elevating them somehow from the imperfect scribblings of a schoolboy to the considered wisdom of
an author. Fifteen years earlier, Napoleon's father had witnessed the same sensation when he printed the first page of
the *Zephyr*—an event he claimed was the greatest thrill of
his life.

In his conquest of the typewriter, Napoleon was instructed, encouraged, and cajoled by Martha, who imparted her
greatest wisdom in the process: Patience and perseverance,
she taught him, are tools that allow one's native intelligence
to unravel the complexities of any challenge.

When he was thirteen, Napoleon took his first wage-
paying job after school let out—as a laborer in the coal
mines. Though he never specified how long he held the job,
his tenure was undoubtedly brief. It was back-breaking, dangerous, dirty work. Laborers were completely at the mercy of
their foremen and the mine's management for both their jobs
and their safety. They had virtually no chance for promotion.
Napoleon's pay was a paltry one dollar per day, half of which
the youth had to pay back to the company for room and
board.

If Napoleon had any lingering doubts about abandoning
his education for the dubious gratification of an income in
the coal mines, they were erased the next year. Protracted
labor strikes erupted throughout the eastern coal mines.
There had been many such strikes before, but never so widespread and never so angry. The anger festered into violence,
the violence into bloodshed. A climax of sorts was reached
in 1897 when deputies in a Pennsylvania coal-mining town
slaughtered twenty striking miners. The miners ultimately
won an eight-hour day, semimonthly pay, and an end to company stores, but Napoleon had already seen enough. His first
brush with working as a laborer was his last. He saw mine
labor as a life of futility and gained what he considered

absolute proof of the wisdom of Martha Hill's homilies about education and acquiring a profession.

While his experience in the coalfields provided a negative reinforcement for Martha's teachings, at about the same time Napoleon also got his first clear vision of how resourceful, determined people can rise above their circumstances.

It began when his stepmother dropped her false teeth one day, breaking the brittle plate. With cash in desperately short supply and the nearest dentist more than a day's ride away, the accident was more than an inconvenience—it was a calamity. James Hill, however, was accustomed to solving such happenstances, having spent his entire life in a wilderness environment that demanded near-total self-sufficiency of its tenants.

"My father picked up the pieces," recounted Napoleon, "placed them together in the palm of his hand, looked at the reassembled plate for a minute, then remarked, 'I believe I could make a set of teeth.' "

"I really believe you can," said Martha.

He was as good as his word. He carved her a temporary plate from wood, and the Hills sent an order to a dental supply house to get the materials for a proper bridge. In his unpublished autobiography, Napoleon recounted coming home from school some time later to find his father attending "a queer looking kettle" heating over the kitchen stove.

"When I asked what it was, he informed me it was a vulcanizer," wrote Hill. "It contained a set of artificial teeth he had just made for my stepmother. . . .Very soon the plate was removed from the kettle, sandpapered down to a finish, and placed in my stepmother's mouth. Believe it or not, it fit almost as well as the plate she had broken; so well, in fact, that she wore it for several more years."

As remarkable as that incident was, it didn't end there. At Martha's urging, James responded to a three-line newspaper ad that read, "Fill your own teeth. For fifty cents will send enough material to fill twenty."

"I gave the order," James recalled decades later, "and received two knitting needles flattened at each end, and a small bottle of mercury and some metallic powders."

From this humble beginning, James Hill, father of four, blacksmith, printer, farmer, and mountain merchant, launched a new career as a self-proclaimed, self-taught dentist. As his business blossomed, he made his own, improved dental implements in his blacksmith shop and ultimately sent off for a twelve-hundred-page book on the subject.

As Napoleon watched with growing wonder, James Hill built a far-flung dental practice even as he learned. He was the only dentist in Wise County and for many miles around and he took the unprecedented step of making house calls—throughout southwestern Virginia and even into eastern Kentucky. He endured long, lonely sojourns into the Appalachian wilderness, attended many who could not pay, and had brushes with the sort of backwoods desperados he had once feared Napoleon would become. But he persevered and won the trust and gratitude of nearly all he met. And the Hills began their rise from poverty.

James Hill's newfound success made it possible for the Hills to change their lives in another way. Late in the 1890s, the family moved from James's cabin to a frame home on a small farm at the edge of Gladeville. The town was later renamed Wise and made the county seat. Well known and well liked, James and Martha settled into their new home ready to prosper and prepare their children for successful lives of their own.

But success would not come easily or linger patiently for the elder Hills—or for Napoleon.

During the time James was building his bootleg dentistry practice, Napoleon was mounting a prodigious professional effort of his own. At the tender age of fifteen, he put his typewriter to use by covering Wise County as a freelance newspaper stringer.

Even in remote western Virginia, he had many potential customers for his work. The various panics and depressions of the late nineteenth century had inspired the formation of the Farmers' Alliance, a forerunner of the farm co-op, founded to establish stores, supply farm implements, and create newspapers for farmers. Virginia was one of the Alliance's strongholds, and small rural newspapers abounded, each desperate for news to print from sources it could afford.

Into this void stepped fifteen-year-old Oliver Napoleon Hill, a willing reporter who knew his way around the hills and hollows of Virginia's most remote farmland and who was already seeking an alternative to a life of drudgery in the fields or coal mines.

Like James's dental practice, Napoleon's initial foray into journalism was inspired by Martha Hill, who first encouraged the boy to write stories about events and people in the surrounding area. She suggested that he send his stories to a weekly newsletter that was circulated to a variety of small newspapers as a sort of rural wire service.

Napoleon soon became a prolific source of stories. His writing was unpolished, if not crude, but he compensated with unbounded verve and a vivid imagination. Indeed, he later recalled that when news was scarce and there weren't stories to tell, he simply made them up.

Friends and neighbors were willing to give the teenager plenty of latitude in his reporting. He was, after all, a reformed tough whose typewriter was far less daunting than a pistol. But there were limits to their tolerance, and, characteristically, Napoleon reached those limits in relatively short order. One of his stories—about a neighbor's moonshining operation—was all too factual and picked up by several newspapers. It brought a squadron of revenue agents into the hills, and in their wake came the moonshining family, massed at the Hill family's front door in a seething fury. In the course of the tense confrontation that followed, they delivered a simple message: If Napoleon ever wrote another word about their moonshining operation, they would throw him and his typewriter into the river.

Although young Nap, as he was called, never again aroused the ire of the backwoods folk with his writing, his penchant for finding trouble in the mountain community had at least one more chapter to go. Not long after the moonshining incident, a raging father came to the Hills' home claiming Napoleon had gotten his daughter pregnant. Napoleon's protestations were not nearly convincing enough to overcome the accusations of the girl or the murderous intent of her father. With head-spinning suddenness, Napoleon found himself married and an expectant father— at the age of fifteen.

Napoleon was devastated. His schooling was over. His writing would give way to work in the fields or mines. His marriage was a sentence to a life of poverty and squalor, a crushing end to his fantasies of wealth and fame and escape from a mountain culture in which he had never—and would never—fit.

But fate—or perhaps James and Martha—provided Napoleon with an unexpected reprieve. Shortly after the wedding, Napoleon's bride confessed that he had not fathered her child. With his exoneration came an annulment of the marriage, and a renewed opportunity to achieve all that he wanted from life.

Thus saved, Napoleon was able to attend a two-year high school when the Hills moved to Gladeville. High school attendance was by no means an automatic progression in turn-of-the-century Wise County, but Napoleon needed no prodding from his father and stepmother to continue his education. Concentrating on lessons was never easy for Nap, but he worked gamely at it. Though he would often say he made it through high school "by the skin of my teeth," he and the other Hill children were remembered decades later by one teacher as "the talent of the school."

Napoleon's diligence and the coincidence of time produced a richly symbolic transition in the year 1900. As the sun rose on a new century, Oliver Napoleon Hill turned seventeen years old, graduated from high school, and left Wise County to attend business school in Tazewell, Virginia. Tazewell was less than a hundred miles from home down the Clinch River, and Napoleon would return to Wise many times in the new century—but only to visit. Napoleon began the twentieth century, in effect, by removing himself from the life he had led and the only place he had known in the nineteenth century.

The Tazewell school's one-year curriculum included basic bookkeeping, shorthand, and typing, preparing students for secretarial work, the traditional entrée into American business and commerce at the time, even for tycoon-minded young men like Napoleon. And Napoleon absolutely bristled with ambition. He had no intention of returning to Wise County as anything less than a strutting, acknowledged success.

As his graduation from business school neared, Napoleon set his sights on working for Rufus Ayres, a prominent attorney who had served as Virginia's attorney general and then became an active promoter for the state's southwestern coal fields. By 1901, Ayres was one of the most powerful and influential men in the region. His firm managed a number of banks and coal mines and he personally held ownership interests in many of them. Ayres was the perfect definition of what the Hills and their neighbors meant when they spoke reverently of "big men." Napoleon could not do better—to start—than to win the attention and favor of this giant.

To realize his ambition, Napoleon sat down and composed an audacious letter to Ayres, one calculated to get his attention. The favor would come later.

"I have just completed a business college course and am well qualified to serve as your secretary, a position I am very anxious to have," wrote Hill. "Because I have no previous experience, I know that at the beginning working for you will be of more value to me than it will be to you. Because of this I am willing to pay for the privilege of working with you.

"You may charge any sum you consider fair, provided at the end of three months that amount will become my salary. The sum I am to pay you can be deducted from what you pay me when I start to earn money."

Ayres admired the young man's style and quickly hired him—with pay. Working out of Ayres's office in Big Stone Gap, Napoleon was an instant success. He came to the office early, stayed late, and worked tirelessly in between. He was an excellent bookkeeper, fastidiously accurate and willing "to go the extra mile to render more service than compensated for"—an axiom that would one day become one of his principles for success.

For Napoleon, the first months of employment with Ayres were a glorious success. The job brought prestige and respect, and he was achieving everything he had hoped to in his most ambitious fantasies. Indeed, as Napoleon became familiar with the business, he began to exhibit the take-charge attitude that told Ayres his new employee was management timber. And Napoleon did everything he could to foster that image. He eagerly took on new responsibilities. He performed his work with enthusiasm and decorum. And he compensated for his youth and five-foot-six stature by adopting the appearance of a serious young executive: ram-rod-straight posture, impeccable double-breasted suits, immaculately pressed white shirts, conservative bow ties, and white handkerchiefs neatly posed in the breast pocket. In less than six months he was promoted to chief clerk at a coal mine in Richlands, some fifty miles east of Wise.

Hill's tenure at Richlands produced the first of many bizarre episodes that would affect his life. He seldom, if ever, discussed this one publicly, yet the incident and the moral dilemma it created stayed in his thoughts for the rest of his days.

As Napoleon told the story in his unpublished autobiography, the incident started when the manager of the coal mine and his brother, the cashier of Ayers's bank in Richland, went on a drinking spree one weekend. The spree came to a tragic end at a hotel when the cashier dropped a loaded revolver that discharged, killing a black bellboy.

"I heard about the accident almost immediately," wrote Hill, "and went quickly to the hotel where it occurred and interviewed the only eyewitness.

"I then called the coroner and procured a burial permit for the negro, together with official recognition of the death as being accidental, and paid the expenses of his burial."

In the course of taking charge, Napoleon learned the cashier had left the bank the previous day and had not returned since. Hill scurried over to the bank and "found it unlocked, the vaults open, and the money scattered around as if a cyclone had hit." He wired a report of the incident to Ayres and was instructed to take charge of the bank, count the money, and charge Ayres's personal account for any shortage.

Napoleon was well aware that Ayres had almost literally given him a license to steal. "I could have appropriated fifteen to twenty thousand dollars or perhaps more without the slightest indication I had taken the money," wrote Hill, ". . . and the opportunity was one which caused me to weigh it carefully." But while Napoleon had his share of human frailties—and would suffer for some of them during his life—outright dishonesty was not one of them. He faithfully counted the money, balanced the books, and discovered that not a cent was missing.

Rufus Ayres was both relieved and incredulous at young Hill's honesty and his handling of the situation. He appointed Napoleon to replace the manager of the coal mine on the spot. In a whirlwind three-day period a nineteen-year-old prodigy from deepest Appalachia took charge of three hundred and fifty men and became the self-proclaimed "youngest manager of a mine in the country."

In his memoirs, Hill used the incident to point out the pragmatic virtues of honesty, since he not only received a handsome promotion but widespread publicity—publicity that cleared the way for his next calling. But Hill would also be affected throughout his life by the ease with which a black man in 1902 Virginia could be killed and buried. He may not have been bothered by this at the time—his entire life had been spent in a community that considered blacks inferior— but he would become an outspoken critic of prejudice and racism long before it was fashionable.

Managing a coal mine was everything Napoleon Hill could want to achieve . . . for a while. He reveled in his newfound authority, his solid income, his stature in Richlands and back in Wise County. But he was and would ever be a restless, seeking man, never content for very long with where he was, always driven to scale new heights no matter how precarious the climb.

As Napoleon began searching for new alternatives from his lofty position in Richlands, he became increasingly drawn to Rufus Ayres's profession. Ayres himself encouraged young Hill to study law when it became apparent that Napoleon could never realize his full potential in a family firm where two sons would always occupy the top management positions.

The thought of counseling clients and swaying juries had great appeal for Napoleon. As a mine manager he found that he loved to advise people and to have people seek his advice. He loved to speak to groups of people, loved the surge of power he felt when he could change their minds and lead them. These were urges that might well have formed during his Sundays in the Three Forks of Powell River Primitive Baptist congregation, watching with a mixture of fear and awe as the most respected members of the community rose to provide all with guidance and judgment. Lawyering offered a way to satisfy these urges and command prestige and wealth in the process.

As Napoleon weighed the merits of a new career in law, two events probably helped him make up his mind to proceed. First, his younger brother Vivian had decided to attend Georgetown Law School in Washington, D.C. Second, his father, having been put on notice by state authorities for practicing dentistry without a license, quietly announced that he was going to dental school in Louisville, Kentucky—at age forty. Napoleon's pride could not allow him to sit idly while a sibling achieved something he also wanted to do, and James Hill's example seemed to demonstrate with clarity that a determined person could reach out and grasp anything American education had to offer.

Not only did Napoleon decide to attend law school with Vivian, he also boasted that he would pay the expenses for both of them by working for Robert L. Taylor, a former governor of Virginia who published *Bob Taylor's Magazine.* The magazine was part of a flourishing genre providing inspiration and guidance for those of modest circumstances who were intent on achieving wealth and power. Its stock in trade was articles about successful people. Taylor had become aware of Napoleon because of the publicity surrounding his success in Richland and agreed enthusiastically when the self-assured young man proposed writing a series of success profiles.

Alas, what started out with such promise lasted less than a year. Law school required long hours of isolated concentration, sheer torture for the peripatetic young man. Worse, the meager earnings of a freelance writer didn't begin to support the lifestyle to which Napoleon had become accustomed in the halcyon days of his management career. Finally, Napoleon told Vivian he would have to find his own way, then dropped out of law school and took a job as sales manager for a lumberyard.

Napoleon Hill's story could well have ended with that move. Already blessed with managerial skills, he quickly displayed instinctive abilities in selling—an outgrowth of his passion for leading and advising people. These tools, combined with his characteristic drive and energy, brought rapid success. The lumberyard's business volume picked up quickly and Napoleon was made a partner, at age twenty-two.

The good times rolled for the better part of two years. Napoleon was well off, respected, and widely admired by young women as one of the community's most desirable bachelors. He himself wondered in his later years whether he would have ever left his comfortable circumstances had not fate given him a shove.

But fate did intervene. Early in 1907, there was a flurry of nervous selling on the New York Stock Exchange, and stock values began a precipitous decline. As the year wore on, companies and shareholders went under in growing numbers. By autumn, even many of the most stalwart American business institutions were reeling. The Knickerbocker Trust, a major New York bank, failed; George Westinghouse's Electric and Manufacturing Company went into receivership, its stock at $90 a share, down from $162 in 1906. The ensuing run on banks put a premium on cash; institutions charged 4.5 percent just to provide currency, and interest rates on loans briefly reached 125 percent.

Napoleon's business hung on grimly through 1907. But when America's economic chaos continued into 1908, the lumberyard was wiped out—and with it, Napoleon's ease and contentment. A man who had already achieved phenomenal success twice by the age of twenty-four suddenly found himself flat broke with no job, no prospects, and no particular place to go.

Stunned but not beaten, Napoleon wasted no time with self-pity. He reviewed his options and immediately eliminated the coalfields, small-town life, or any semblance of a step back toward his roots. He wanted to put himself in the big picture: big cities, big business, a big future. His best ticket, he decided, was *Bob Taylor's Magazine*. It didn't offer the income he sought, but it would locate him in cosmopolitan Washington, D.C. His work would expose him constantly to the movers and shakers of American commerce. He would surely find a path that led to the grand heights his brief business career had promised.

He agreed with Taylor to focus his profile work exclusively on the giants of industry and business. Taylor would open the doors, using his contacts and influence to schedule the interviews, and Hill would enter. Both men would benefit—Taylor receiving the immense prestige and circulation impetus of exclusive interviews with the greatest names in American business, Napoleon prospecting for the golden opportunity he knew awaited him.

In the autumn of 1908, Hill set out to rebuild his life. His father had recently graduated with honors from dental school, his brother Vivian from law school. Both embarking on new careers of great promise while the family's original prodigy, just weeks away from his twenty-fifth birthday, arrived in New York City with barely enough money in his pocket for the return trip home.

But it was a sense of adventure, not humiliation, that Napoleon felt as he made his way to an immense estate on the northern fringe of bustling Manhattan, where his first major interview was to take place. Standing at the entrance, he straightened his jacket, squared his bow tie, took a deep breath to calm his nerves, then knocked.

As the butler opened the massive door to Andrew Carnegie's majestic home and ushered him in, Napoleon Hill was overwhelmed with wonder and excitement, and with the sense that what was about to happen to him would change the course of his life.

CHAPTER 3

1908–1918

The greatest among men are those
who serve the greatest number.
—Napoleon Hill

Never before in Hill's life had he encountered firsthand such prodigious wealth. The young man was awestruck as the butler escorted him through the baronial splendor of Andrew Carnegie's four-story, 64-room mansion on upper Fifth Avenue in New York City. In 1908, the north end of Manhattan was still semirural, and the great industrialist's sumptuous residence sat on a vast expanse of hill that looked out onto scenic vistas more typical of countrysides than cityscapes.

As a nervous Napoleon Hill was ushered into the vast library-study, he was immediately greeted by the steel magnate himself. The short, stocky seventy-four-year-old Carnegie, white hair and white beard neatly trimmed, smiled warmly as he got up from his famous rolltop desk, which was so massive it was said to have been constructed inside the room. The study itself was formidable; thousands of books lined the shelves, and the walls were covered with Carnegie's favorite proverbs and aphorisms. Hill never forgot the one that Carnegie was particularly fond of and had given a place of prominence on the wall. It read:

He that cannot reason is a fool.

He that will not is a bigot.

He that dare not is a slave.

Hill may not have realized it on that fateful day, but he had finally met his mentor. What he did know, however was that he admired everything about Carnegie: the poor immigrant Scottish boy, barely educated, who started out as a messenger for a telegraph company and rose to become—by the time he was thirty-five—one of the country's empire builders, creating America's steel industry and amassing an extraordinary fortune. But beyond Carnegie's "Horatio Alger" life—the personification of the American Dream come true—was yet another aspect of the man that deeply impressed Hill. In fact, it would eventually become the cornerstone for Hill's own philosophy of success. This was Carnegie's spiritual nature—his faith, his deep and abiding belief that "the greatest service one can render to God is by helping others." This passionate desire to serve humanity was the foundation for Carnegie's lifelong and immense philanthropy. By the time he died in 1919, he had already given away over $350 million—over $2 billion in today's terms. It's likely that his noble example inspired in Hill the beliefs that would become manifest many years later in his own magazine, in its pages preaching the philosophy of "service"—of helping people—as the finest goal to which one could aspire.

Listening to the great man expound on his "principles of achievement" was an enlightening experience for Hill. "The richest heritage a young man can have is to be born into poverty," Carnegie told him. He saw his own humble origins not as a deterrent to success but rather as the inspiration to overcome all obstacles and attain seemingly impossible goals. If one had a strong sense of self-worth, Carnegie claimed, no degree of impoverishment could hold one back. "Individuals who achieve outstanding success are not born with some peculiar quality of genius not possessed by others. Confidence is a state of mind. It is under the control of the individual, not an inborn trait. And the starting point for developing that self-confidence is definiteness of purpose." This was Carnegie's cardinal rule in his philosophy of personal achievement. "The man who knows exactly what he wants, has a definite plan for getting it, and is actually engaged in carrying out that plan, has no difficulty in believing in his own ability to succeed. Only the man who procrastinates soon loses confidence and winds up doing nothing."

"But what happens," Hill asked, "when a man knows what he wants, has a plan, puts it into action and meets with failure? Doesn't that destroy his confidence?"

Carnegie smiled. "I hoped you would ask that, because it is important to understand what I'm about to tell you. I believe that every failure carries within it—in the circumstances of the failure itself—the seed of an equivalent advantage. If you examine the lives of truly great leaders, you will discover that their success is in exact proportion to their mastery of failures. Life has a way of developing strength and wisdom in individuals through temporary defeat."

But Hill persisted. "Most people aren't going to believe that every failure has an equivalent advantage when they are overcome with the adversity. What does one do if the experience destroys one's self-confidence?"

"The best way to guard against being overwhelmed by failure," Carnegie said, "is to discipline the mind to meet failure before it arrives." He spoke of the need to take full possession of one's mind. The mind, he said, was the true source of infinite power. One's dominating thoughts created one's being—one's persona. In contemporary language, it might be expressed as, "You become what you think about." Carnegie illustrated his theory by recalling that as a laborer fifty years earlier, he had overheard a fellow worker saying, "I hate poverty, and I'll not endure it." Carnegie told Hill that the man was still a laborer because he had fixed his mind on poverty and stopped there. "But if the man had said, 'I enjoy riches and shall earn and receive them,' he would have been disciplining his mind to focus on those goals, which he could then achieve—rather than simply hating his lowly station in life" (the cornerstone of the principle that Napoleon would later identify as a "positive mental attitude").

"It would have helped, too," Carnegie added, "if he had gone one step further and described what sort of service he intended to give in return for the riches he deserved." Carnegie used the birth of his country as an example of the power of men's thoughts. "One reason why we Americans are the richest and freest people in the world is the fact that we think and talk and act in terms of freedom and riches. Our nation was born out of our desire for liberty, and we thought and talked so much about it—became so obsessed with it— that we were ultimately able to fight for it and achieve it." But, as he explained, it couldn't have happened if the Founding Fathers hadn't had a very clear goal in mind. "Our country was forged by men who had a definite purpose and vitalized it with a burning desire to achieve that purpose. Men of great achievement form the habit of making an obsession out of their definite major purpose."

Carnegie went on to expound on another of his theories: the mastermind alliance. He believed that John Hancock, Samuel Adams, and Richard Henry Lee had created just such a union—mostly through correspondence—by communicating their hopes and dreams of freedom for the Colonies. And it was this passionate sharing of their ideas and ideals that eventually led to the historic meeting at Independence Hall "where fifty-six men signed their names to the document that gave birth to a free nation: the Declaration of Independence."

"Was it really that simple?" Hill asked.

"It was far from simple," Carnegie replied, "but the principles at work are simple. Of course many secret meetings of this first Continental Congress had to be held in order to turn their definite major purpose into action. But it was from this highly concentrated effort—in which these men visualized their new and liberated country—that the inspiration came for Washington's soldiers to fight and triumph over almost insurmountable odds and achieve that glorious end."

Carnegie saw that his words were having profound effect on Hill, that the young man was more than just a good listener who appreciated an old man's wisdom. He sensed in Hill a perceptive mind and an intense desire to learn, to achieve. This pleased Carnegie so much that he told Hill he was inclined to let their talks continue beyond the allotted interview time. And thus it was—much to Hill's stunned surprise—that the industrialist invited him to spend the entire weekend at the mansion. For Hill this opportunity to exchange ideas and theories with Carnegie was a golden one, and he welcomed it with gratitude. Their conversations over the next couple of days would become, three decades later, the basis for Hill's most famous work, *Think and Grow Rich!*, the best-selling and most influential self-improvement book ever written. For the rest of Hill's life—in books, speeches, seminars, and lectures—he would continue to write and talk about the "remarkable Mr. Carnegie" and what had transpired on that memorable weekend in 1908.

As they strolled through the millionaire's lush private gardens, Carnegie told Hill that by learning to control one's thoughts, one has the privilege of building one's own character. The mind, he said, is the source of all happiness and all misery, of both poverty and riches, the builder of friendships, the creator of enemies. It has no limitations, save only those which the individual imposes on himself through his lack of faith. "Truly," he said, "whatever the mind can believe, the mind can achieve."

Hill said, "That's very inspiring—but most people seem to lose that faith in themselves somewhere along the way. Or they never find it in the first place."

Carnegie replied, "That's true. Regrettably, with all this miraculous power available, the majority of people allow themselves to be cowed by fears, doubts and self-imposed limitations. My early days of youth were cursed with poverty and with limited opportunity; a fact with which all who know me are acquainted. I am no longer cursed by poverty because I took *possession* of my mind, and that mind has yielded me every material thing I want, and much more than I need. But this power of the mind is a universal one, available to the humblest person as it is to the greatest."

What's more, Carnegie told Hill the lives of Ford, Edison, Rockefeller, Firestone, and Alexander Graham Bell were all similar to his own, and it was through their trial-and-error experiences, their definiteness of purpose and their decisive actions—"for without action, plans and aims are fruitless"— that they earned the success, wealth, and fame they now enjoyed. Even more exciting to Hill was Carnegie's conviction that the average person—if he wanted to improve his own life—could do so by studying the lives of such great leaders. Whether they were industrialists, presidents, inventors, or religious leaders, the commonality of their stories could enlighten, inspire, and benefit the entire world. All it would take, Carnegie believed, was sharing that knowledge— the philosophy and the steps to success—that had been gained by those who had achieved greatness. Carnegie knew this could be a priceless gift to millions of people: an opportunity to learn from those who had started out no differently than any other ordinary person, but had through the infinite power of their minds transformed their lives and the lives of millions of others.

Carnegie felt this project would require extensive interviews with hundreds of leaders from every walk of life, as well as studying the lives of those great leaders who had passed on, compiling all the information and research and distilling it into a comprehensive set of principles. This tremendous undertaking, he said, would require at least twenty years to complete. The book that came from it would serve as a tool to help people everywhere to help themselves, and enable them to realize their dreams. Hill confessed that he not only shared Carnegie's utopian vision, but believed it could be accomplished.

That was exactly what Carnegie wanted to hear. With his usual bluntness, he turned to Hill and, without any further preamble, inquired if he felt equal to the challenge of undertaking this great work himself. Hill was honored—and amazed—that Carnegie saw in him someone worthy of the task. But Napoleon Hill believed he *was.* It took him less than half a minute to accept the offer. In fact, it took exactly twenty-nine seconds, according to Carnegie, who had taken out his stopwatch and was timing Hill's response. Afterward, he told Hill that he had given him a maximum of sixty seconds to come to a decision. If it had taken even one second longer than that, Carnegie said, the offer would have been withdrawn because "a man who cannot reach a decision promptly, once he has all the necessary facts, cannot be depended upon to carry through any decision he may make." Carnegie himself was famous for making his decisions quickly and never going back on them, never regretting or worrying about them later on.

Hill was relieved that he had passed the test. But he wasn't prepared for the shock that followed. Andrew Carnegie's enormous project involved absolutely no financial remuneration whatsoever, apart from reimbursement for out-of-pocket expenses. Hill could hardly believe this piece of news. Here was one of the richest men in the world offering to one of the poorest an assignment that would take twenty years of diligent work, and he wasn't going to pay a dime for it. Carnegie assured the astonished Hill that the rewards from this labor would be far in excess of any payment he might offer, that Hill would be learning the secrets of success first-hand and that doors would be opened to him that he could never have opened for himself. Finally, and most importantly, Hill would have the privilege of giving to the world one of the most enlightening documents ever written. In fact, Carnegie predicted its publication would undoubtedly bring Hill great success for himself. Of course, the young man wanted to do it—it was the most potentially enriching opportunity he would ever have—but he wondered silently, almost in horror, how he would be able to sustain himself through the entire endeavor. But that was Carnegie's offer, and it would never change. Neither would Hill's acceptance of it. Swallowing his pride and his fear, he accepted the assignment with gratitude, humility, and almost uncontrollable excitement. Years later when he reflected on that day, Hill described it as the time when "the Hand of Destiny reached out to me."

The Hill family's reaction to the project on which Napoleon was about to embark ranged from mild skepticism to derision to outright anger. With the possible exception of his stepmother, Martha, they all agreed that it was a foolhardy decision and believed firmly that it would be impossible to carry out this project and earn a living at the same time. They were giving voice, of course, to Hill's own inner doubts, but all the scoffing around him only fueled his determination to go through with the assignment. Obviously Andrew Carnegie's first principle for success—to have a definite major purpose—had, at least subconsciously, taken hold in Hill's own mind.

By the end of 1908, someone else would come into Hill's life who would change it forever. It was during the snowy December of that year that he met Florence Elizabeth Hornor, a pretty young woman from Lumberport, West Virginia. They were both living in Washington, D.C., at the time—Florence caring for a young niece who had polio, and Hill with his brother Vivian, who had finished law school and was now starting practice. Napoleon was writing for *Bob Taylor's Magazine* and at twenty-six was still a long way from anything resembling success in his professional life, but on the personal side, Florence Hornor soon brought to Hill a happiness he had never known before. Though she was in her senior year of high school, Florence was already twenty years old, having delayed the start of school for several years, probably due to family responsibilities. An excellent student, she was about to graduate with honors, spoke fluent German, had a thorough knowledge of chemistry, and had brilliant English language skills.

Napoleon met this remarkable young woman unconventionally—like almost everything else he did—because of a classified ad he had placed in the Sunday edition of the *Washington Times.* It read: "Educated refined young businessman, who just moved to Washington, would like to meet refined young lady, preferably not over 18 years old, object mutual friendship with possibility of leading to matrimony; answers strictly confidential, and if desired, would meet any member of girl's family first and convince them of my good intentions and personal standing in my home town. Address: Young Southerner, Box 27, Times Office."

It wasn't the reserved Florence who answered Napoleon's ad, but a cousin who lived in the same house. When Napoleon was invited over for a get-acquainted visit, however, it was Florence who caught his eye and his heart when she came into the parlor to retrieve some schoolbooks. She and

Napoleon took one look at each other and it was quite literally love at first sight.

Ten years later, Florence wrote about that evening. "I came downstairs looking for those books and found my future husband instead, or rather he found me, for when he saw me and I began to retreat back upstairs, he came and brought me down." She found Hill intensely serious and overly dignified, and decided to somehow, someday make him *smile*. She referred to him as her "Prince Charming," and there's no doubt he was equally smitten, for she recalled that Hill told her, "God must have sent me here especially to meet you." A few days later, on their first date together, Napoleon poured out his heart to Florence, told her not only about his past—all the grim childhood years in the backwoods of Virginia—but also about the golden future he envisioned for himself: a life of lofty accomplishment and service to humanity. That was all Florence needed to hear. "I made up my mind then and there that I would marry him and help him realize those dreams," she later wrote.

Within a year of meeting, Napoleon and Florence became engaged—without her family's knowledge or consent, probably in order to avoid whatever objections the Hornors might have had to such an announcement. After all, as bright, ambitious, and energetic as Napoleon was, he still had no money and a very uncertain future, and the Hornors owned not only property but a number of successful businesses in and around Lumberport. Reluctantly, Florence consented to this "secret" engagement, but she was unable to refrain for long from breaking the news to her mother.

Flora Hood Hornor had already met Napoleon Hill about six months earlier when she was on a brief trip to Washington, and she liked the earnest young man. But Florence knew her mother would be upset and wrote a reassuring letter declaring her deep love for Napoleon and her faith in their future. And then she prevailed on her fiancé to do the same.

On plain stationery that bore a large handwritten letter *H* tilted rakishly at an angle in the upper-left-hand corner, Hill wrote:

> My dear Mrs. Hornor:
>
> I write a great many business letters every day, and I usually know just what I wish to say and how to say it before I started to write, but in this instance, I must confess that the letter I am beginning to you finds me without knowing what to say, how to begin or when to stop. I am very glad that I met you when you were here last year, as the short acquaintance I had with you during your short visit has at least equipped me with the knowledge that you are a good hearted, broadminded Southern lady, which tends greatly to make me feel that the object of my letter to you, even though the letter itself is poorly constructed, will be considered with only that courtesy and consideration which any good Southerner might extend to another.
>
> Of course Florence has told you of our engagement, and this effort on my part to become more acquainted with you will not therefore come as a surprise and I trust not as a disappointment. I know that you, as most mothers, will feel more or less reluctant to have your little girl leave you to assume the duties and responsibilities of married life, but I know you realize that this is a condition only natural and one which usually confronts every mother of a daughter when she has grown up to a mature age.
>
> When Miss Florence returns home this summer, I hope to have the pleasure of becoming more intimately acquainted with you all.
>
> > Very sincerely,
> > Napoleon Hill

Flora Hornor was often described as the gorgon of the family, feared and hated by almost everyone, but her reply to Hill's letter was sympathetic and no more than understandably concerned. And she apparently found endearing Napoleon's genuine desire to be accepted and approved, especially since he had expressed it with a disarming guilelessness that allowed her to convey an honest and touching maternalism.

> Dear Mr. Hill,
>
> Your letter came a few days ago, and in reply, I want to say that Florence has told me that you and she are expecting to be married. As you say, it is not a pleasing thing to know that I have to give up my daughter, but this has come as such a surprise to me that I can hardly accustom myself to the idea. Florence is nothing more than a child. She is the youngest and has always had her way. Now, Mr. Hill, I am looking out for Florence's happiness and have no objection to the marriage if you feel you can be happy together. She is a dear, good child, so affectionate, and has always been so kind and thoughtful to her mother. I feel sometimes that I can hardly bear this, but I want to consult her happiness and do what is for the best. I can't say that one of my children is dearer to me than the other, but she has always been with me and studied my happiness more than the others, consequently, I will miss her more. I do think you should know each other and be in no haste. I am very anxious to see more of you, to know you better and have you meet the rest of my family. You must come this summer and make us a visit.
>
> Hoping to see you soon, I am,
>
> > Very sincerely,
> > Flora Hood Hornor

Whatever period of engagement Flora Hornor would have preferred, her wise counsel went unheeded. On June 23, 1910, the headstrong couple were married, and Napoleon—contrary to Flora's wishes—came to meet the rest of the Hornors *after* he had become a member of the family. Fortunately, they liked Florence's new husband and were impressed with his intelligence, self-confidence, and energy.

Besides, he not only adored his bride but was full of grand plans and promises for their life together.

The newlyweds set up housekeeping in a tiny apartment in Washington, D.C., making only occasional visits to Florence's family in Lumberport, but there was one visit that was never to be forgotten by the Hornors—or, for that matter, the entire town of Lumberport.

It was a cold, rainy November day in 1910. Florence was staying at her mother's house—she had come back to see the family doctor to confirm what she had suspected for several weeks now, that she was pregnant. Napoleon was on his way to join her for the obligatory visit with his mother-in-law. The Baltimore & Ohio Railroad line, he knew, did not extend into Lumberport because there was only a rickety wooden bridge across that section of the West Fork River, and he would have to traverse the last three-mile stretch of road on foot. But it was raining when he got off the train, and by the time Hill arrived at the Hornor home, mud-splattered and soaked to the skin, he looked more like a vagrant than Florence's dapper young husband. Hill was so incensed that he complained to Florence's uncle, V. L. Hornor, head cashier at the Lumberport Bank, about the deplorable road conditions. Hornor agreed that transportation to and from the town was a disaster, but he explained that no one was willing to pay for a real bridge. Although Lumberport had been trying for ten years to get one built, he said, only a trolley company was willing to finance it and they simply didn't have the one hundred thousand dollars needed for construction. So the new bridge remained unbuilt and the roads remained a mess.

Hill took Florence's uncle to the riverbank and pointed out that the county road which crossed the wooden bridge was creating a dangerous intersection for the B&O Railroad on the other side, because its tracks were often blocked by traffic on the bridge. Therefore, Hill reasoned, the B&O

should be willing to contribute to the building of a new bridge. And so should the county commission, he went on, since it would be providing much safer and more serviceable roads. It would even stimulate the economy and help to bring new business into Lumberport, he pointed out persuasively. Hornor was clearly impressed with the young man's logic and enthusiasm. Hill said he had an idea: Why not have all three enterprises—the railroad, the county commission, and the trolley company—join forces and share in the cost of the bridge?

It was a plan worth pursuing. Hill immediately gathered together a committee consisting of several prominent towns-people, the local councilmen, and Lumberport's mayor, and he set up a meeting with the division superintendent of the Baltimore & Ohio Railroad. After explaining the hazardous conditions, Hill asked the railroad to finance one-third of the new bridge's construction. The superintendent thought it was a fair request and agreed to it. The county commission was equally willing to put up another third, and the trolley company came up with the rest. Construction was soon underway and in less than six months, Lumberport's long-dreamed-of bridge had become a reality. It accomplished all the needed ends and even fulfilled Hill's prediction that it would bring economic benefits to the town. Lumberport began thriving as it had never done before. Hill could take pride in what he had accomplished, and years later he would use it as an excellent illustration of one of his success "laws": combining a definite purpose with an immediate plan of action. It was also probably the very first time that Hill had used his considerable skill as a motivator to bring people together and create a spirit of cooperation and desire for creative change. Justifiably impressed with young Napoleon, the Lumberport citizenry even went so far as to nickname him Andrew Carnegie, *Junior.* Hill basked in the flattering comparison.

Thirteen months after he and Florence were married, their first child—a son they named after Hill's father, James—made his entrance into the world. In their Washington apartment, the Hills had now become a cozy little family, full of parental pride for their new offspring. Hill had just returned from a trip to Detroit, where he had gone to interview Henry Ford, who would one day put that city on the map—and America on wheels. Carnegie had given Hill a letter of introduction to the car manufacturer, and Hill was excited about the opportunity to meet him.

"But I must confess," Hill wrote many years later, "the meeting with Ford was disappointing. He was cold, indifferent, unenthusiastic and spoke only when forced to." Hill persevered, however, and although he never felt he got anything worthwhile from Ford himself, he did talk to many of the men working in the plant, as well as local merchants and business associates of Ford. Hill found no one who shared Carnegie's estimation of Ford, which was that the man would one day be considered a genius. But Carnegie's prophecy did come true, and Hill acknowledged this several decades later when, upon reflection, he realized that Ford did indeed possess at least one or two of the essential ingredients for extraordinary success: iron self-control and the ability to concentrate all one's efforts on attaining one's goal. At the time Hill met with him, however, Ford didn't want to talk about the principles of success, he just wanted to talk about his *car.* And when he did, according to Hill, it was the only time that Ford "loosened up." In fact, he proudly showed off the recently introduced Model T, and gave Hill a brief lesson in operating the car by taking him for a spin around the factory. Hill loved it so much that he bought one himself—for the considerable sum of $680—and drove back to Washington to surprise Florence with his new acquisition.

She was probably not only amazed but also aghast over her husband's extravagant expenditure. Florence's dowry

money was fast running out and, now that there was a growing family to support, Napoleon could no longer ignore the
reality of their financial plight. He badly needed a steady
means of income.

Whether by luck or design, in the wake of his meeting
with Ford, Hill soon landed a sales job with an automobile
company in Washington, D.C. He brought to this new line of
work his usual blend of diligence and enthusiasm, and
undoubtedly did far more than he was paid to do (a trait that
would one day translate into his principle of "going the extra
mile—rendering more service than you're being compensated for"), with the result that he was soon responsible for a
steady rise in the company's profits. And within a few more
months, Hill was building up the company in another way:
He had instituted an "educational" department—even calling it The Automobile College of Washington—where he
trained chauffeurs and car owners to drive and prepared
mechanics to hold assembly-line jobs in automobile plants.
Certain that he could realize even greater profits for the company, Hill confidently arranged for credit from a local bank to
finance the expansion of the company.

The banker he was dealing with may have realized that
Hill's naïveté in money matters could easily be exploited, but
Napoleon was also undoubtedly equally responsible for what
happened next. His expectations were simply unrealistic, and
he was too anxious to get ahead too fast. Hill began borrowing heavily from the bank, became overextended, and soon
found himself unable to keep up with the payments. In a last,
desperate attempt to save the floundering business, he borrowed from Florence the enormous amount (in those days)
of four thousand dollars. But even his wife's help was in vain.
The bank took over the company, and Hill no longer had a
job. It was a difficult and painful lesson for him, and there
would be many more in a lifetime of setbacks and come-
backs, before he would begin to understand why the setbacks

had happened. And perhaps he never did completely comprehend his own role in these unfortunate affairs—his own failings both as a businessman and as a judge of character.

Although the money Hill borrowed was Florence's own to do with as she pleased, the Hornors knew that what they had just witnessed did not bode well for her future, or that of her new family. Still, they were not unforgiving. They, too, knew the difficulties and vicissitudes of owning one's own business, and they didn't condemn what happened, nor were they quite ready to condemn Napoleon either. After all, his almost singlehanded skill in arranging for the financing and building of the Lumberport bridge had led them to expect great things of him, and they were still hopeful. But they prayed that, in the future, Hill would be more careful about whom he dealt with and what kind of enterprises he became involved in.

For now, they were sympathetic about the venture's failure and willing to come to the Hills' financial rescue. Through the Hornor and Hood family connections, they were able to arrange for Napoleon to go to work in what he would later describe as "the easiest job I ever had." He and Florence and the baby left Washington and moved back to Lumberport, where Hill became an assistant to the chief counsel of the Lumberport Gas Company, a Hornor-owned family business. It is likely that Hill's rudimentary legal background helped in justifying him for the position.

But Hill wasn't happy with his new work. He used to say he was comfortable in it and well paid—and extremely bored. The job offered no challenge to the ambitious young man, and there was an "inner voice"—a feeling he couldn't shake—that told him he wasn't doing whatever it was he was meant to do. It gnawed at him, made him irritable and frustrated and often depressed. He wanted to do something that he could feel was more his own, more true to himself. Certainly the Carnegie project filled that need, and he did work on it in his spare time—researching, reading, and studying the lives of successful men—but, of course, as always, it provided no income. Florence beseeched him to keep the job, if for no other reason than that she was pregnant again, and their ever-growing family needed even more economic stability. But her voice was no more than a whisper compared to the one that Napoleon heard in his own mind. He had already decided to quit the job—as soon as his second child was born.

But nothing could have prepared the young couple for what they would discover when they first saw their new son shortly after his birth on November 11, 1912. Napoleon Blair Hill was born with a physical handicap that was to become a source of obsessive concern—but ultimately of inspiration—for Napoleon Hill. The baby boy was not only born deaf; he was completely without ears. In the years to come, despite intense fighting with both family and schoolteachers, Napoleon would never allow the boy to learn sign language. He was determined to singlehandedly teach his deaf son to speak—and even to hear. As the boy was growing up, Hill would talk to him for hours with his lips pressed against Blair's cranial bone at the base of the neck, just behind where his ears would normally have been. Years later the boy did begin to hear, for it was discovered that the bone itself was conducting sound to his brain. And eventually he wore a specially designed hearing aid that dramatically improved his hearing and speaking abilities.

But it was Napoleon who inspired Blair's desire to overcome his handicap. The father never allowed his son to give up; he didn't even allow Blair to consider himself handicapped. Hill taught his son that deafness was simply an adversity that could be triumphed over. It engendered an abiding mutual trust between Hill and the boy. Many years later, in a letter to Florence attempting to buoy her spirits about their own future, Napoleon wrote, "I often think of the faith little

Blair always had in me. Remember how he used to say 'Daddy knows how' with a sparkle in his eyes." Because of Blair's challenge, as well as his sweet disposition as a child, he was constantly spoiled by the Hill and Hornor families and grew up to be "everyone's favorite," the most beloved member of the family.

When Blair was still an infant and little James was a year and a half old, true to his promise, Napoleon left his cushy job in Lumberport as assistant to the corporation lawyer. Despite Florence's reasonable objections, he was determined to venture off in search of greener pastures. And he was sure he couldn't find them in Lumberport. Hill acknowledged that it was a perfect place to raise the children, but he himself really didn't like small-town life. Only a big city held the promise of excitement, adventure, and success that he dreamed of. He wanted someplace that would challenge him, and he chose Chicago. He wrote, "I believed it to be the most competitive field in the world, and that if I could gain recognition there I would prove to myself that I had material in me that might someday develop into real ability." Hill was always ready to test his mettle.

In late 1912 he packed his bags, said a tearful good-bye to his wife and baby boys, and boarded the train to Chicago. This journeying off to seek his "rainbow's end" was the beginning of a pattern that would be repeated many times during Napoleon and Florence's marriage, and ultimately, Hill's family life was the price he would pay for wanting to make his own way in the world, and do it on his own terms.

Soon after arriving in Chicago, Hill came across a want ad for LaSalle Extension University, which needed someone to work in its advertising and sales department. Believing that it held great promise, he applied for the job and, once again, Florence's family helped him secure the position. George W. Atkinson, a former governor of West Virginia and then a judge in the U.S. Court of Claims in Washington, was a friend of the Hornors and, at their request, wrote a letter to the vice president of LaSalle. Dated December 18, 1913, it read:

Dear Sir,

Answering your inquiry in relation to Mr. Napoleon Hill, I can say that he is a young man full of energy and enthusiasm, and has had much experience as a business advertiser. He is not only energetic, but he is very resourceful. I feel quite sure he will prove adaptable for the sort of work you desire.

I do not feel that you need have any fears as to his integrity or reliability, as I know nothing against him in that respect.

If you employ him, you will find him ever ready to carry out your wishes and, if necessary, he will work early and late to perform the duties you assign to him.

Very respectfully,
G. W. Atkinson

This glowing recommendation helped clinch the job. After the easy boredom of his job in Lumberport, this new post sounded to Hill like an exciting challenge. But even more satisfying was the underlying sense that he just might be on the right track this time, inching closer to what he *should* be doing. The only difficult—and wrenching—part had been leaving Florence and the babies behind. But there simply wasn't enough money to support his family's living with him in an expensive city like Chicago, and Hill knew the uncertainties that lay ahead were more than they should be subjected to. He felt consoled knowing Florence was in familiar and loving surroundings with her entire family to watch over her and the children. Of course, she was unhappy about the separation, and Hill had to assure her that he would be sending for them just as soon as there was enough money to do so. Someday, he promised, they would live in a lovely big home with beautiful gardens, servants, cars, the finest schools for the boys, a world for all of them that—if only in his mind—would be nothing short of paradise.

Soon after Hill went to work in the advertising and sales department at LaSalle, he had stationery printed that bore the letterhead: "Napoleon Hill, Attorney at Law, 2715 Michigan Avenue, Chicago," and in the lefthand corner it read: "Dept. of Law, LaSalle Extension University, Attorney for the Lumberport Bank, Lumberport Gas Company." This highly exaggerated claim looked impressive on paper, but there is no record of his having actually performed legal services for anyone. Hill was more active, fortunately, in his legitimate capacity as an advertising salesman, and as a teacher of advertising techniques to other salesmen. He began doing very well, and by the end of the first year wrote home that he had earned $5,200, which was a great deal of money in those early years of the twentieth century. Ecstatic over his financial success, Hill wrote, "The shining pot of gold is almost within my reach." But until he had that "pot" firmly in his grasp, Hill wasn't quite ready to send for his wife and children. At least there seems to be no other explanation for why he wouldn't have brought them to Chicago at this point, for this salary he boasted of would have been more than enough to support them. He may have had doubts, of course, about whether he could earn that kind of money on a consistent basis. But the other possibility is that Hill inflated the amount he earned.

Salary aside, Hill was gaining invaluable insight into what it was he liked doing, and what he did well. He had a natural gift for teaching people how to sell—products, service, and, above all, themselves. His ability to motivate others began to emerge as a powerful tool during this period at LaSalle. In the years to come, he would hone these skills even further, eventually becoming a "grand master" in the art of motivation. Hill, a man in search of a mission, was finally beginning to circle around that mission. What made him so good at what he did was nothing more or less than inborn talent. He had all the basic qualities: genuine enthusiasm, a deep desire to help others realize their own goals, and a sincere belief that their dreams and wishes deserved to be fulfilled. Hill also worked very hard to instill in the salespeople he taught the one quality he had in abundance—a strong sense of self-confidence. It was important to him to pass along the vital lesson he had learned from Andrew Carnegie, that the only limitations are those people place on themselves. Slowly but surely, Hill was beginning to create his own philosophy of success. And much of what he was teaching came from what he himself was learning by working tirelessly on the Carnegie project. Whenever there was time, he would spend it writing letters, sending questionnaires, interviewing and analyzing the lives of hundreds of people. Both the knowledge he was gaining and his own determination to carry on the research combined to keep the endeavor alive no matter how daunting it often seemed to be.

Although there is no evidence of discord between Hill and his employers at LaSalle, he decided to strike out on his own again after less than two years. His next enterprise seemed to hold the promise of lucrative expansion. In writing about it many years later, Hill explained that he "purchased a half interest in an operating franchise of the Martha Washington Candy Company." With three other partners he helped to reorganize the company, renamed it The Betsy Ross Candy Company—"Betsy" after the diminutive for Elizabeth, Florence's middle name—and made candy using recipes directly from his wife's kitchen. According to Hill's third son, David, his mother had always had the gift of making the most delicious chocolate candies.

With himself as president, Napoleon felt the company's success was assured—and it *did* begin to expand and grow. The partners opened Betsy Ross Candy Shops not only in Chicago, but in Baltimore, Milwaukee, Indianapolis, and

Cleveland. Hill was suddenly riding high on the crest of his most successful enterprise thus far. "I had at last found the business in which I wanted to remain for life," he wrote. At the close of 1914, he printed up a Christmas proclamation in which he spoke of the inspiration his family had provided in his efforts to be "a successful businessman, a patriotic American and a humble Christian." Among his good fortunes he also counted "citizenship in a country that is free from war and where national strength, wealth and power are used as mighty influences for peace." In a final paragraph, his goodwill overflowed: "I have no fault to find with anyone on earth. . . . if I have done any good deeds during 1914, I hope to double them during 1915. If I have been useful to any human being during the old year, I hope to be doubly useful during the New Year." And he also promised that "I shall not pass into the year 1915 without seeing my dreams of a national chain of Betsy Ross Candy Stores near complete realization."

Looking back on these last words, the irony was surely not lost on Hill, for the new year brought a bitter end to his presidency of the candy company and his dreams for its future. To put it mildly, Hill's three business associates weren't fond of him, and their dislike was probably not without provocation. Hill was a man who had what his son David described as "a hell of a temper," one that wasn't hard to set off. He also had an ego that required a great deal of recognition. Some forty years later, one of his closest friends and associates, W. Clement Stone, who always admired and respected Hill, nevertheless said, "He could be very difficult to get along with if people didn't see things his way."

Hill's business partners obviously didn't see things his way at all. One of them not only wanted him out of the company entirely, but demanded that they receive Hill's interest in the business without paying for it. "I balked more stiffly than they had anticipated at this request," said Hill. "To gently urge me toward the 'grand exit,' they had me arrested on a false charge and offered to settle out of court if I would turn over my interest in the company." What that "false charge" was remains unknown, but Hill wrote that he insisted on going to trial. When the time arrived, however, and no one was present to prosecute, the presiding judge threw the entire case out of court, according to Hill, with the statement that "this is the most flagrant case of attempted coercion that has ever come before me."

Hill was vindicated, but in an effort to restore his good name, he sued his ex-partners for fifty thousand dollars— damages for malicious injury to his reputation. Five years later, the case finally came up in Chicago's Superior Court, and Hill said "a heavy judgment was secured." But years before this favorable decision was rendered, recalled Hill, the partner who had originally sought to depose him was already in the federal penitentiary, convicted of another crime. And one of the other partners was "out of business and in disgrace." Not only was there vindication at last, but Hill saw at work something he would refer to in later years as the Law of Compensation. It was based on one of Hill's favorite biblical prophecies: "Whatsoever a man soweth, so also shall he reap." Hill never believed that more firmly than he did then.

He also saw this calamity as still another test of his faith. "I sometimes wonder," he wrote, "if it were not well for all of us to undergo these experiences which try our faith and exhaust our patience, and cause us to lose control and strike back, because we learn, in this way, the futility of hatred and envy and selfishness and the tendency to undermine the happiness of a fellow human being." Philosophical about his financial losses, he wrote, "What a blessing it is when we come to the realization that everything which we accumulate in the way of material wealth will finally become as useless as the dust to which our bones will return." But the sad reality was that the end of his tenure in the candy company had left Hill out of work and flat broke.

This unfortunate turn of events once again wreaked havoc on his family's welfare. Florence was still a loving and devoted wife, but the capriciousness of her husband's business affairs and his inability to support his family—let alone live with them—was beginning to hurt her deeply. She would have to turn again to her own family for both monetary and emotional support, and that must have been difficult for her. Florence also found herself more and more in the position of having to defend her husband to both the Hornors and the Hoods. They had begun to distrust Napoleon Hill, and it was an attitude that was progressively reinforced through the coming years.

Was Florence being "conned" by her own husband? The Hornors were beginning to think so. Their concern for Florence and their growing wariness toward Hill made it more and more uncomfortable for everyone when he came to visit the family in Lumberport. Inevitably, these visits became infrequent during the next decade. But if the Hornors had now become disenchanted with Florence's husband, he wasn't enamored of them either. In all likelihood, he probably resented them for their judgment of him and envied both their business holdings and their respected position in the community. In any case, it was only Florence who remained staunchly loyal. Napoleon was, after all, the loving father of her young sons and, when he was around, an adoring husband. And often, in letters written to her after they had been married twenty years, he would still sign them, "Your Lover." Whatever he may not have been, Napoleon Hill was unquestionably an incurable romantic.

The Betsy Ross Candy Company debacle came as a terrible blow to Hill. He had believed fiercely in its potential for growth and ability to bring success for himself. But he still longed as deeply as ever to savor the joy of having it all—the money, the fame, the sense of great accomplishment. Even when—with almost perverse regularity—his business ventures failed miserably, either within a couple of years or a couple of months, Hill refused to collapse along with them. He considered them only "temporary defeats," no more than a test of his faith and a spur to keep on trying.

In the wake of this latest reversal, Hill decided to take a closer look at what it was he could really do best. His talents in advertising and salesmanship were still his strongest suits, so he chose to make use of them once again. But this time with a difference. Hill decided to go it alone, in a solo enterprise, so that he could have more control over his work and its destiny. Where he got the capital for his venture is a mystery, but it probably took very little initial investment, and the likelihood is that another loan from Florence covered his expenses to launch the George Washington Institute, a correspondence course in salesmanship.

The course consisted of a long series of typewritten "Lessons," in which Hill preached at length on everything from "truth in advertising" to "knowledge of the 'self' " to the "principle of service." "When we begin to help others," he wrote, "we begin to help ourselves . . . in proportion to our service to the world do we ourselves succeed." After studying and analyzing, by his count, "over 10,000 men and women who were earnestly seeking their proper niche in the world's work," he had concluded that self-confidence and enthusiasm were the key prerequisites to success—especially for salespeople. But Hill went far beyond sales techniques and motivational pep talks. He was beginning to plumb the underlying *psychology* of success. In one lesson he wrote, "Upon reflection, I seriously doubt that such a thing is possible as failing to get what one really wants. The truth of the matter is that you are either consciously or unconsciously getting *that which you think about most intensely.*"

Autosuggestion, he told his students, is a powerful tool for disciplining the mind. "It brings you what you order!" he wrote. One must be careful, therefore, in deciding *what* to order. And once you decide specifically what it is you want, what kind of person you want to be, "write down a description of it, memorize it and then affirm it to yourself at least a dozen times a day, stating it forcefully and, if necessary, to an imaginary person." It was Hill's fervent desire to have his students learn who they were, to "find themselves" through the course. He wanted them to expand their consciousness and use *that* to get whatever they wanted in life.

In another lesson, he expounded eloquently on the necessity of feeling love and charity toward others, even if they may have wronged one in some way. "Sow the seeds of kind and loving thoughts," he wrote, "and they will take root where thistles grew before. The world is a great looking glass in which we see not the imperfections of others as we imagine we do, but the thoughts and actions which we create ourselves."

By 1917—a year after it began—the George Washington Institute was earning Hill a modest income, and he proudly noted the first anniversary in one of the lessons. "Last night our resident class held its commencement exercises at the Chicago Advertising Club. More than a hundred people were in attendance at this farewell meeting. It marked the closing of the hardest year's work I ever performed. . . ."

But Hill's euphoria was soon washed away by the apocalyptic tide of history. For almost three years now, the First World War had been raging all across Europe while the United States remained neutral, watching in horror as the German kaiser and his howitzers decimated the Continent. But then, in April 1917, after the sinking of several U.S. ships, President Woodrow Wilson announced a declaration of war against Germany. In Hill's "Lesson #30" he wrote of this sad day, headlining it with the famous quote: "Those who live by the sword, die by the sword," and then went on to say, "As I write, there are being mobilized in America millions of men and billions of dollars to bring home this great truth to an autocrat on the other side of the Atlantic who started to rule the world by the sword some three years ago. Sometimes it requires the shedding of much blood and devastation of great fortune to impress this truth upon those who deny it but in the end, the truth still prevails!"

Hill's patriotism didn't stop there, for he wanted to *do* something, to more actively participate in the war effort. So he wrote to President Wilson and offered his services in whatever capacity he might be useful. The two had met years earlier when Wilson was president of Princeton University and Hill had come to interview him with a letter of introduction from Andrew Carnegie. Apparently Wilson never quite forgot the intense and highly motivated young journalist. Since Hill was foremost a writer, Wilson offered him the job of creating propaganda material for use in industrial plants and places of business where war machinery and goods were being manufactured. Hill accepted the assignment—without pay. He later wrote, "President Wilson wanted to place me on the government payroll at a rather attractive salary, but for once in my life I had the privilege of vetoing the President of the United States. Thus, I assigned myself a job which made it essential that I go the extra mile, with no thought of what I might receive for my services."

Fortunately, the war had not yet taken its toll on Hill's George Washington Institute, and Hill boasted proudly that "despite the ravages of war, my school was growing by leaps and bounds." Inspired, perhaps by the notion of public service as a result of his association with President Wilson, he used one of his lessons for the Institute to put forth an extraordinary proposition. After a passionate denunciation of what he believed were the deplorable inadequacies in the American public school system, Hill stated that what he was teaching his adult pupils should also be taught to young children, for they could learn at a very early age to develop honesty, self-confidence, and positive moral values. All of which made excellent sense, of course, but he proposed to achieve this worthy goal by taking matters into his own hands. Hill exhorted his pupils to "sit down this very day" and write letters to six leading Chicago newspapers urging them to back Napoleon Hill in "his race for a seat in the United States Congress." With the support of his student body, he hoped to acquire the legislative power to pass laws that would impart to children "an understanding of the working principles of their minds!"

When this ardent appeal met with little or no response, Hill's political ambitions soon waned, and the George Washington Institute went back on course again. And it kept going—still modestly—until a second military draft, early in 1918, "practically destroyed my school, as it caught most of those who were enrolled as students. At one stroke I charged off more than $75,000 in tuition fees and at the same time was contributing my own service to my country."

The autumn of 1918 should have been a time of joy for Hill. Florence was due to give birth to their third child, and Germany was at last being defeated throughout Europe. The war, mercifully, was drawing to a close. But Hill's spirits were extremely low. The Institute was now barely operating, Hill's work at the White House was winding down, and the Carnegie project continued to drag on, year after year, demanding his time and energy without producing any revenue whatsoever. Carnegie's words of a decade earlier drifted back to him: "The job will require twenty years, during which time you must be willing to starve rather than quit." But he also remembered Carnegie saying that if he could see the assignment through to the end, the result of all his selfless labor would be "the world's first philosophy of individual achievement." These words had sustained Hill through a number of bleak moments when he was almost ready to give up the project, to admit that his family was right after all and their prophecy had come true: He couldn't earn his way in the world and still do justice to the overwhelming endeavor that had been bestowed on him.

Hill had already done a great deal of the research work. He had sent questionnaires and written letters to hundreds of prominent people and received many valuable responses. Famous and successful people all over the country had shared their experiences and insights with him, some even in person. He had interviewed Henry Ford and Cyrus Curtis and Thomas Edison and Woodrow Wilson. He had learned their secrets for success, learned how they handled their setbacks and failures, learned how their minds worked. The more he studied and compiled the information, the more he was certain that the message was a vital one, and that the world deserved to hear it.

But there were times—and now was one of them—when he didn't have even a modest income to tide him over, when he was totally unable to care for his wife and sons, when he felt that the Carnegie project would never be finished. But still, he never gave up—or stopped working on it for more than short periods of time. His inner voice, he told Florence, kept him going, telling him it would all be worth it one day. But she herself was an inspiration to keep at it. She had supported him unconditionally from the beginning; she knew his talents; she shared his dreams.

On October 26, 1918, the day Napoleon Hill turned thirty-five, he received the sweetest birthday present of his life—his third son, David, was born. The baby was healthy, and his parents could not have been more grateful.

Shortly after David's arrival, James Monroe Hill, Napoleon's father—who was now working as a dental surgeon in Wise, Virginia—wrote a letter to his daughter-in-law in proud, grandfatherly tones.

"Dear Flossie & the boys," he began. "I trust that all is

going well and that you are the mother of some great states-
man or president-to-be, the generation of tomorrow. Such is
not at all impossible.

"I sometimes wish I could buckle up a strip of the earth's
crust and bring our homes closer together, so I might play
with the boys every Sabbath afternoon. I could get so much
more out of life by being thus surrounded with the second
crop from the old tree."

James was also grateful that the war was coming to an
end, referring to the Germans as "a stench in the nose of
democracy," and somberly acknowledged that "the price of
liberty comes high; the blood of many noble sons has paid
the debt." He mentioned, too, that Napoleon's brother Vivian
was now serving in Europe as a second lieutenant in the
army, and he expressed his concern about the flu epidemic
that had swept through the Continent and had now reached
America, "visiting your town like ours and swelling the casu-
alties to a prodigious number." But he ended on a happier
note of love: "Tell Jimmie and Blair that I am going to send
old Santa around to see them at Christmas. And to that other
little precious piece of humanity as well."

Although James and Martha Hill didn't see as much of
Florence and their grandchildren as they would have liked,
the Hills' relationship with their daughter-in-law seemed to
grow stronger through the years, while the one with their son
Napoleon continued to deteriorate. Geographical distance
certainly played its part, for Hill simply was almost never
home. But beyond that, James Hill had begun to feel that his
son should have found a way by now to provide more fully
for his family and to get them all living under one roof. He
would become angry when he thought of Florence, separat-
ed from her husband most of the time and raising the boys so
much on her own. Unlike his son, James was equally fond of
Florence's family, and was concerned that Napoleon might be

taking advantage of their goodwill and generosity. It made for a deepening estrangement between father and son.

Despite Hill's many doubts and fears about his work—and his future—he was at least temporarily distracted by being with his family, especially with its latest addition. And both six-year-old Blair and seven-year-old James were thrilled to have their daddy home with them. He took the boys for long walks in the woods, taught them birdcalls, and showed them how to shoot pigeons—he was still a crack shot—all the while instilling in them an understanding and appreciation of nature that only a man who spent his childhood so close to it could have done. Florence nursed her infant son, baked her delicious cakes and candies, watched her husband play with their two boys and prayed secretly that this could go on forever. But she knew Napoleon had to return to Chicago to close down the correspondence school for good and to go, one last time, to phase out his job in Washington.

Hill was in the White House on the day in early November that the Germans requested an armistice. "I was sitting in President Wilson's office," Napoleon later wrote, "as he read the decoded message from them. His face turned white as snow. When he finished reading he handed the document to me and left the room. He was gone for about fifteen minutes. When he returned, he handed me a couple of sheets of paper on which he had written his reply to the Germans, which ended with three questions related to the terms of the armistice. After I read his reply, he asked if I had any suggestions to add to it. I said, 'Yes, Mr. President, I would suggest a fourth question. I would ask whether the request for an armistice has been made on behalf of the German people or the German war lords.' 'Of course,' exclaimed the President, 'for that will put them on notice to get rid of their Kaiser before they can get an armistice.' And it did just that." On Armistice Day, November 11, 1918, Hill wrote, "The slaughter has ceased, and reason is about to reclaim civilization once more."

Although he felt jubilation and relief that the war was over, Hill's worries about his own welfare were weighing on him heavily that day. He was not only broke—once again— but a man very much in search of one of his own principles of success: a definite major purpose. It was certainly eluding him. Hill went back to his office and stood looking out the window at the street below as it swelled with growing crowds of people joyously celebrating the armistice. As he watched the rejoicing parade surge along, his own life passed in review before him. He began taking stock—the bitter with the sweet—and realized that he was at a crossroads, a time in his life when something important was meant to occur. Unsure what it was supposed to be, or how he could make it happen, Hill proceeded to do the only thing that had never failed him—the only thing he knew how to do really well. He began writing. He sat down at his typewriter, and the words started pouring out, faster than he could type them. He wrote feverishly, not planning or even thinking about what he was putting on paper. "I just wrote whatever came into my mind!" Hill recalled. But he did admit that "unconsciously I was laying the foundation for the most important turning point of my life." He began with the day's historic announcement:

> The war is over!
>
> Soon our boys will be coming home from the battle-field of France.
>
> The lord and master of brute force is nothing but a shadowy ghost of the past!
>
> Two thousand years ago the son of man was an outcast with no place of abode. Now the situation has been reversed and the devil has no place to lay his head.

Let each of us take unto himself the great lesson that this world war has taught: namely, only that which is based upon justice and mercy toward all—the weak and the strong—the rich and the poor alike, can survive. All else must pass on.

Out of this war will come a new idealism—an idealism that will be based on the Golden Rule philosophy; an idealism that will guide us, not to see how much we can "do our fellow man for" but how much we can do *for* him, that will ameliorate his hardships and make him happier as he tarries by the wayside of life.

And while I am intoxicated with the glorious news of the war's ending, is it not fitting that I should attempt to do something to help preserve, for the generations to come, one of the great lessons to be learned from William Hohenzollern's effort to rule the earth by force?

I can best do this by going back twenty-two years for my beginning. Come with me, won't you?

It was a bleak November morning when I got my first job as a laborer in the coal mining regions of Virginia at wages of a dollar a day.

A dollar a day was a big sum in those days; especially to a boy of my age. Of this, I paid fifty cents a day for my room and board.

Shortly after I began work, the miners became dissatisfied and commenced talking about striking. I listened eagerly to all that was said. I was especially interested in the union organizer. His words fascinated me. Standing on a dry goods box, in the corner of an old shop where he was holding a meeting, he said:

". . . Men, we're talking about striking. You want more money for your work and I want to see you get it. May I not tell you how to get more money and still retain the goodwill of the mine owner? We can call a strike and probably force them to pay more money but we cannot force them to do this and like it. Before we call a strike, let us go to the owner and ask him if he will divide the profits of his mine fairly with us.

"If he says yes, as he probably will, then let us ask him how much he made last month and if he will divide among us a fair proportion of any additional profits he may make if we all jump in and help him earn more money. He will no doubt say, 'Certainly, boys, go to it and I'll divide with you.'

"After he agrees—as I believe he will if we make him see we are in earnest—I want every one of you to come to work with a smile on your face; I want to hear you whistling as you go into the mines. I want you to go to work with the feeling that you are one of the partners in this business.

"Without hurting yourself, you can do almost twice as much work as you are doing. If you do more, you'll help the owner make more money. And if he makes more, he will be glad to divide a part of it with you. He will do it for sound business reasons, if not out of a spirit of fair play.

"If he doesn't, I'll be personally responsible to you and if you say so, I'll help blow this mine to smithereens! That's how much I think of the plan, boys. Are you with me?"

And they were, to the man!

The following month, every man in the mines received a bonus of 25% of his month's earnings. Every month thereafter each man received an envelope with his part of the extra earnings. On the outside of the envelope were the words: *Your part of the profits from the work which you did that you were not paid to do.*

I have gone through some pretty tough experiences since those days twenty odd years ago, but I have always come out on top—a little wiser, a little happier, and a little better prepared to be of service to my fellow men, having applied the principle of performing more work than I was actually paid to do.

I believe most earnestly that anything a man acquires from his fellow man without the full consent of the one from whom it is acquired, will eventually burn a hole in his pocket, gnaw at his conscience until his heart aches with regret.

Hill paused, and then resumed typing, amazed at what he found himself writing:

To get this philosophy into the hearts of those who need it, I shall publish a magazine to be called *Hill's Golden Rule.*

It takes money to publish national magazines, and I haven't very much of it at this writing; but before another month shall have passed, through the aid of the philosophy I have tried to emphasize here, I shall find someone who will supply the necessary money and make it possible for me to pass on to the world the simple philosophy that lifted me out of the dirty coal mines and gave me a place where I can be of service to humanity. The philosophy which will raise you, my dear reader, whoever you may be and whatever you may be doing, into whatever position in life you may make up your mind to attain.

You can get along with little schooling, you can get along with but little capital; and you can overcome almost any obstacle if you are honestly and earnestly willing to do the best work you are capable of, regardless of the amount of money you receive for it.

Within a week of writing this essay, Hill took it to George Williams, a Chicago printer whom he knew through his White House work on wartime propaganda material.

Williams was familiar with Hill's writing and agreed to see him immediately. As Hill sat in his office, Williams read the document carefully, then looked up and smiled at Hill. "You prepare the copy, and I will print the *Golden Rule* magazine and place it on the newsstands."

Hill was elated. He fairly danced out of Williams's office. Not only was this going to be a wonderful Christmas present for his whole family, but Hill now realized—with a clarity of vision he'd never experienced before—that he was finally on the threshold of truly embarking on his mission in life. He would now be able, for the first time, to get his message across to people everywhere. The seeds of the philosophy of success were about to be sown, and the "laws" he had been formulating and distilling would soon transform not only his own life but, ultimately, the lives of millions all over the world. Hill's rainbow was never more vivid, his pot of gold growing ever closer.

CHAPTER 4

1918-1927

For the United States and millions of its citizens, life would never be the same after World War I. On the streets and in the fields, there was chest-thumping pride in the country's military might. In the boardrooms and factories there was the heady knowledge that the young nation possessed the world's strongest and fastest growing economic machine.

It was a time of wonder and hyperbole. Wonder that global dominance on the battlefield could be won by a nation that had spent the previous six decades waging war primarily on itself—North versus South, frontiersman versus Indian, cattleman versus farmer, capitalist versus laborer. Wonder that a nation previously perceived by the starched aristocracy of Europe—and by itself—as a ragtag society of dispossessed immigrants and unwashed adventurers could suddenly find itself the world's dominant industrial power. Nothing like 1918 America had ever existed, or so it seemed to postwar Americans. They had freedom and plenty. They had strength and righteousness. And they had a lofty position in the world's hierarchy of nations.

Tens of thousands of war-weary soldiers returned to

civilian life in America, bringing with them visions of European cities and cultures and mores and morals. For many, a return to dirt farming and rural living was out of the question. These veterans were joined by tens of thousands more who had flocked to the nation's industrial centers to fill wartime jobs and had neither the desire nor the means of returning to the small towns and homesteads that produced them.

So it was with the Hill family. Napoleon's brother Vivian returned from Europe where he had served as an officer and took up a practice in business law in Washington, D.C. Paul Hill, Napoleon's half-brother, entered medical school, eventually to become a surgeon. Both brothers would become very successful in their careers, both would remain unmarried the rest of their lives, and both became cold and distant to the other members of the Hill clan.

Napoleon, of course, had severed his ties with small-town and rural living long before World War I. Perhaps the only option he did not consider in the waning days of 1918 was remaining with Florence and the kids in Lumberport, West Virginia, the town Florence could not and would not leave. But unlike his brothers, Napoleon's passions were building—for his wife, his family, his work, and, ultimately, for creating and communicating his gospel for success.

Hill's Golden Rule was an outlet for something that had been building inside of Napoleon Hill since he had been old enough to feel the spiritual vibrations from the preachers and elders who made the Three Forks of Powell River Primitive Baptist Church crackle with emotion and exhilaration. Even as his obsession with achieving material success had led him from the Appalachia backwoods into mining, lumber, retail confections, and automobile sales, another obsession was growing even stronger within his soul. He wanted and would finally *need* more than anything to lead, to lecture, to advise

. . . to electrify great gatherings of followers, and to minister by the spoken and written word to the masses. His goal was the fame his stepmother had described when she swept into his life. His message blended biblical psalms and gospel with the lessons of Carnegie, Edison, Ford, and dozens more modern-day apostles of success. His style was a unique blend of the disparate cultures he represented: the vocabulary and sentence structure was ornate Eastern establishment, while the delivery sparked with the pointed anecdotes and passionate imagery of a Primitive Baptist sermon.

Conceived on November 11, 1918, the first forty-eight-page issue of *Hill's Golden Rule* was written, edited, printed, and delivered to newsstands in early January—a whirlwind start-up even for a large, sophisticated publishing house. The size and the sophistication of the force behind *Hill's Golden Rule* was limited to a single editor—Napoleon Hill—and the print-shop resources of George Williams.

"Having no funds with which to employ outside writers," Hill wrote in his memoirs, "I wrote every word of the material for the first edition, changing my style on each article and using various pen names to cover my identity." Indeed, Napoleon would write and edit nearly every page of the first nine issues, even many of the advertisements. In addition, he would make dozens of unpaid personal appearances each year: To boost circulation, *Hill's Golden Rule* offered free Napoleon Hill lectures and training sessions for employees of companies that purchased bulk subscriptions.

It was a shoestring operation that could not possibly succeed. Napoleon's "style changes" were more apparent to him than to readers. The research and interviews for articles were limited to what Napoleon himself could snatch from daily newspapers—and what he had accumulated from his years of work on the Carnegie project. And the pages of *Hill's Golden Rule,* from cover to cover, issue after issue, streamed from the typewriter of a single, part-time writer: To preserve the magazine's precarious cash flow, Napoleon took no salary and had to support himself and his family with other work. *Golden Rule* was written in the wee hours of dark, lonely nights, in silent isolation on weekends that might have been spent with his wife and children, and on trains that bumped and rocked through America's hinterlands to deliver Napoleon to business meetings and speaking engagements in a seemingly endless blur of great cities and dusty towns.

Hill's Golden Rule couldn't possibly succeed, but it did. The first edition sold so briskly at newsstands that it went to three printings. And, with its cover language always including the legend, "The two little dimes that you invest in this copy may mark the turning point in your career," sales of the magazine grew a little stronger with each new issue.

The magazine's success was a testimony to Hill's talent and perseverance—and especially to his unique editorial concept. America had an endless variety of religious publications and perhaps an even greater selection of business magazines. But *Hill's Golden Rule* was a unique blend of the two, an unlikely combination of moral guidance and secrets to success. The cover story for the May–June 1919 issue, for example, was entitled, "The Greatest Oil Boom In the History of the World, and the Law of Compensation." The rambling six-page article presented one Texas oil-field vignette after another to dramatize how success ultimately comes to those who toil faithfully, while failure forever stalks those who give up.

Interwoven with the vignettes was a highly idealized view of the Texas oil boom. One passage saluted a restaurant that served a fine lunch for fifty cents when the proprietor could easily have charged "five or six times this sum." Hill attributed the proprietor's restraint to sheer human goodness, a desire to earn only a fair profit.

Such goodness was pervasive in the oil fields Napoleon portrayed. "I met more millionaires in Texas than I ever saw in my life before," wrote Hill. "They seemed to be unusually democratic and considerate of others who were less fortunate, a quality that does not always go with the millionaire!"

Hill often wrote of Texas and oil in the magazine, partly because of their interest to success-hungry readers but also because Hill himself was trying to make a living in the oil business while waiting for *Hill's Golden Rule* to produce enough revenue to pay him a salary.

Along with many inspirational stories, *Hill's Golden Rule* published practical self-help articles on topics ranging from writing effective sales letters to a series on using psychology to succeed in business. Like everything else in the issues, these articles were based either on Napoleon's own experiences or his own theories—or both. In either event, his point of view was expressed with assurance and authority, it was supported by human interest anecdotes, and every story, every vignette, every opinion brought the reader back to two fundamental truths in life. First, the Golden Rule—doing unto others as you would have them do unto you—was the best ticket to success in business and in life. Second, success comes to those who set goals and pursue them regardless of obstacles and disappointments.

In its totality, *Hill's Golden Rule* had a cover-to-cover vigor and determination—a raw energy—that could penetrate the resistance of the most determined skeptic. Even those who recognized the magazine's journalistic shortcomings, even those who may have doubted the qualifications of the editor-philosopher at its helm, could not resist the inspiration that came from reading an issue. You can succeed. You can succeed at anything. You can succeed by being worthy of success.

Ironically, Hill himself nearly failed just months after the start of *Hill's Golden Rule.* In looking about for an income-producing job to sustain him through the magazine's start-up period, Napoleon received an offer of "more than $100,000 a year" to organize a company to raise money for oil drilling. He accepted and spent several months in Dallas, Texas, putting together a staff and getting the new company off the ground. Florence and the boys struggled to make ends meet while Napoleon waited for his first paycheck. Alas, the few checks he ever received in the oil business didn't even cover expenses, and one—for $150—bounced. At length, Napoleon discovered that the head of the company was off on wild spending sprees and bilking his investors. The company was nearly insolvent, and the federal government was getting ready to launch a fraud investigation that would encompass the firm and its officers, including Nap.

Napoleon managed to get the company into the hands of receivers to protect its investors, and he was able to extricate himself from any legal entanglements since he had done nothing wrong. But he received virtually nothing of the promised one-hundred-thousand-dollar salary and left Texas in even more dire financial straits than when he had come. Vowing never to get involved in anything like this again, he turned his full attention to the magazine, and from that point on, *Hill's Golden Rule* began to flourish.

Toward the end of 1919, as Hill neared his thirty-sixth birthday, his very soul glowed with the satisfaction of imminent success and fulfillment. The magazine was already generating enough revenue to allow him a salary. He described its circulation as growing "in leaps and bounds." He was still working sixteen hours a day, seven days a week, but, he recalled later, "I was having a glorious time, as any man does when he is engaged in a labor of love."

The magazine's first blushes of prosperity also made it possible for Hill to hire an associate editor, bringing some relief to his nearly impossible workload and making it possible for him to spend time "honeymooning" with Florence.

Napoleon's good cheer was especially evident in his letters to Florence. The expressions of love and affection for her and the children that had marked earlier letters continued unabated, while sentiments of loneliness and melancholy were gradually replaced by cheery reports about his best speech ever, inspirations for profit-making ventures, and blithe visions of shopping Chicago's finest stores to find clothes and furs for his faithful and deserving wife.

And Napoleon was flourishing on another level. His need for personal acceptance and recognition—by great groups of people and by individuals of influence and power—was being realized time and again. One of his favorite memories from that time was an occasion when he traveled to a school in Davenport, Iowa, to deliver a lecture to students and turned down the standard one-hundred-dollar lecture fee as a gesture of goodwill.

"The morning after my departure," recalled Hill, "the head of the school called his 2,000 students together, told them of my refusal to accept the fee and the reason therefore, then requested every student to send at least one subscription to my magazine. During . . . the weeks that followed I received from . . . those students more than $6,000 in subscriptions. . . ."

The Davenport story joined Hill's arsenal of anecdotes about the positive returns that come from giving more than asked—living by the Golden Rule. Another from that same year came when he spoke to a group of Parker Pen employees in Janesville, Wisconsin. George S. Parker himself made the invitation and welcomed Napoleon as a weekend guest in his home. When Hill left, Parker drove him to the train station and delivered a personal message that Napoleon would recall many times during the rest of his life.

"As the train pulled in," Hill wrote in his memoirs, "[Parker] took hold of my hand, placed his arm around my shoulder and said, 'I invited you up here so I could see for myself if you were sincere in your belief in the Golden Rule. Now that I've looked into your heart I have only this to say—you'll never know, as long as you live, of the tremendous amount of good you are doing through your . . . magazine."

Nowhere was Napoleon's effusive goodwill in more abundant proof than in the December 1919 issue of *Hill's Golden Rule.* In an editorial written on his birthday, Napoleon looked back with satisfaction on the experiences he had accumulated over thirty-six years. "My experience has taught me that a man can no more sow a crop of grief and expect to reap a harvest of happiness than one could sow thistles and expect to reap a crop of wheat," he wrote.

In another passage, celebrating the first year of *Hill's Golden Rule,* he exclaimed, "Some of the greatest philosophers, teachers, preachers and business men of the age have not only pledged us their hearty moral support, but they have actually gone out and rounded up subscriptions for us in order to help foster the spirit of good-will which we are preaching."

In still another editorial in the December issue— Napoleon's "Little Visits with Your Editor" column usually included at least four different subjects and filled up to ten magazine pages—Hill urged readers to send Christmas cards to their enemies, to celebrate the victory over the kaiser, and to rejoice that the passage of the Prohibition Act meant "old John Barleycorn [has been] laid away forever."

Of all the sermons, vignettes, and sayings published in the December 1919 issue, none had greater relevance in Napoleon Hill's own life than a maxim displayed on the first page of his column. "Every year I live," wrote Hill, "I am more convinced that the waste of life lies in the love we have not given, the powers we have not used, the selfish prudence that will risk nothing, and which, shirking pain, misses happiness as well." For Napoleon, *Hill's Golden Rule* was a triumph of risk over selfish prudence, and the happiness—a special, heightened sense of happiness that only came with risk—was just beginning.

★ ★ ★

The dawn of the Roaring Twenties marked a new era for Napoleon Hill. He was no longer preoccupied with achieving wealth and power as a business tycoon; he now thought of himself as a writer and philosopher whose genius had created a successful magazine.

There was another, more symbolic transition, too. Hill started the new decade without his great mentor. Andrew Carnegie had died in 1919. Hill's other mentor, W. Clement Stone, was still nearly two decades removed from Napoleon's life. Indeed, as Hill sat down to write his January 1920 editorial, "Thoughts on a Steel Magnate," a teenage Stone was launching his insurance career selling door-to-door for his mother, who had just acquired an agency in Detroit.

It was an independent, self-assured Napoleon Hill who penned the January editorial. It was not a eulogy for Carnegie. In fact, it was inspired by the even more recent death of Henry Clay Frick, Carnegie's partner and archrival in the U.S. Steel Corporation. As if serving notice that his days as a star-struck, hero-worshipping novice reporter were long past, Hill composed four and a half pages of stinging criticism of both men.

"Everything [Frick] did was done in a spirit of cold, unemotional self-aggrandizement," wrote Hill. "His most dominant thought was to pile up dollars and it seems that he cared not at all how or from whom he got those dollars."

Hill went on to suggest that the bitter struggle between Frick and Carnegie for control of U.S. Steel played a role in the labor unrest of the current day. "The fight which [Frick] and Mr. Carnegie waged on each other, in their mad quest of money, undoubtedly served as an example for their thousands of workers to follow. . . ." wrote Hill. "Who is wise enough to say whether or not this example of colossal greed, as portrayed in the life-work of Andrew Carnegie and Henry C. Frick, is largely responsible for the spirit of unrest now being manifested among the steel workers in those mills which they once controlled?"

About his onetime mentor, Hill had this to say: "Mr. Carnegie's record is little better. That which he did for the public in the way of building public libraries was probably done largely as a sop to his personal vanity! Had he quietly donated the money for those libraries without announcing who the donor was, and called them, 'The People's Library,' leaving off the word 'Carnegie,' we might have found more to commend in his action. . . . Poor old man Carnegie!"

Napoleon's broadsides against the likes of Carnegie and Frick were hardly a recanting of his pro-business, pro-success preachings. *Hill's Golden Rule* contained tens of thousands of words each month urging and aiding its readers to succeed in business, and campaigning against anticompetitive elements in American society ranging from organized labor to socialists. But unlike traditional conservatives of the era, who tended to rationalize capitalism's excesses by pointing out that everyone had the same chance to enjoy those excesses, Napoleon was piecing together a populist philosophy that made laissez-faire capitalism far more appealing—and accessible—to the common man. It was a uniquely twentieth-century American twist on the centuries-old European concept of "noblesse oblige." The latter held that the aristocracy was entitled to control wealth and power, but had the obligation to use it fairly and wisely. Hill taught that all people had the obligation to gain success and, having done so, to devote some portion of their lives and fortunes to helping others reach the same goals.

His was a highly idealized philosophy, uniting materialism and morality, capitalism and humanism. His expressions of this philosophy were sometimes built on flawed logic and inevitably poured forth in torrents of overstatement and redundant anecdotes. But for thousands and then tens of thousands of Americans, it worked. It offered hope for those struggling to overcome their life's circumstances, and it offered relief in tense labor relations by urging ambitious wage earners not to strike but to find better opportunities for themselves from the infinite possibilities available in America the free.

Although Napoleon experienced many years where he made more money, 1920 played out like a success fantasy. Public recognition of the man and his magazine swelled. He embarked on a nationwide lecture tour that took him to most of the largest cities in the country. He held large audiences spellbound with his sizzling, rapid-fire delivery. He spread the gospel of success and moral responsibility with the passion and intensity of a true evangelist. He reached the hopeful and the downtrodden. He electrified their senses with pulse-pounding sermons and sent them home with purposeful visions and an absolute belief in their ability to achieve their visions.

Hill's recognition and acceptance mushroomed. One article he wrote advocating that parents send their children to business colleges was reprinted as a pamphlet; so powerful was his endorsement that tens of thousands of copies of the pamphlet were immediately purchased by business colleges around the country for use in their promotions. Indeed, sales of the pamphlet continued for nearly two decades and, according to Hill, reached ten million copies.

But even as Napoleon's career soared to new heights, the seeds of destruction were being sown. He would lose *Hill's Golden Rule* in an internal power struggle later that year. The exact causes for the conflict are far from clear. Hill's own personality undoubtedly played a role. Ever the sharp-tongued critic and pontificating adviser, his lifelong penchant for offending those closest to him expanded in direct proportion to his ego—which in 1920 was being lavishly fed by his success. In addition, his lectures were taking him away from the office and the magazine more and more. His associate editor,

Guy Bilsland, took on an increasing share of the writing load but got little, if any, of the glory, his bylines generally running in the back of the magazine. By August he had apparently moved on to other things.

Meanwhile, publisher George Williams was becoming increasingly concerned about his fast-moving partner and editor. Hill's promise to "create a worldwide service in the interest of the [human] race" had made charming promotional copy in the beginning, but in 1920 it was becoming clear that Napoleon had every intention of pursuing this grandiose vision. For a conservative midwestern printer whose goal was to publish a profitable little self-help magazine, Hill's evolution into a "business evangelist" with all its attendant visions of grandeur was probably too much to swallow.

Adding to Williams's stress was the fact that Hill was becoming a controversial figure thanks to the printed attacks of a rival publisher. Williams began pulling editorial control away from Hill and, with the printing of the October 1920 issue, took full control of the magazine.

Napoleon's own version of the events read like a business soap opera, replete with intrigue, betrayal, and sinister characters from his past. In his memoirs, he focused on a mudslinging campaign against him waged by one Bob Hicks, publisher of *Specialty Salesman,* and the backstabbing activities of one of his own associates, a man named Tom Igoe whom Hill variously referred to as a secretary and an associate editor but who was listed on *Golden Rule*'s masthead as business manager.

His troubles with Hicks began when *Golden Rule* published a story about Arthur Nash, a Cincinnati businessman who had taken his clothing enterprise from failure to miraculous success. "Golden Rule" Nash, as the story referred to him, had reversed his fortunes by treating his employees like partners in the firm rather than as ignorant laborers—by "taking them into the business with him." They responded by doubling and tripling their previous productivity levels.

"As soon as the Nash story came out in my *Golden Rule*," wrote Hill, "Mr. Hicks hotfooted it up to Cincinnati, formed some sort of working alliance with Mr. Nash, and began to exploit him as a Hicks find.

"For years afterward he did the same thing wherever he could in connection with every prominent person whose story I published. Meanwhile he kept up a continuous mud-slinging campaign against me as being little short of the old fellow with hoofs, horns, and spiked tail."

His internal problems, said Hill, stemmed from a power-hungry associate who was somehow allied with one of Napoleon's former students in the George Washington Institute. The former student had a grudge to settle with Napoleon. During his George Washington Institute days, the student had charged Napoleon with fraud. It was a spurious charge, so lacking in substance as to be thrown out of court in the pretrial hearing—but not before the student drummed up damaging newspaper coverage. Never one to accept damage meekly, Napoleon had returned the student's favor by making the FBI and other government agencies aware of his adversary's "suspicious" activities and his thick German accent. In the anti-German hysteria that preceded America's entry into World War I, the student was first put under a blanket of close surveillance, and finally detained for the duration of the war.

While the latter-day "German spy" assaulted Hill's character and integrity, Igoe, his associate, worked on Williams. "[He] was a young fellow whom I had taken out of a job as a day laborer in a steel plant and put to work in our office, to help my secretary while I was away lecturing," wrote Hill. "He took advantage of my absence as a favorable opportunity to poison the mind of Mr. Williams, the printer, by telling him it was not my ability that was causing the magazine to sell so rapidly but the name of the publication itself."

Ultimately, the pressures from within and without pushed Williams to take precipitous action. "Old man Williams collapsed and practically buckled on me," wrote Hill, "despite the fact I had already voluntarily given him a half interest in my magazine. He became so difficult to deal with that I was very unhappy in my relationship with him, but the straw that broke the camel's back came when my young disloyal protégé, who could barely read and write, induced Mr. Williams to alter and edit my editorials and other writings, without my knowledge or consent."

Whatever else may have transpired, when Williams and Hill reached this deadlock it was more than Napoleon could tolerate. "My work was no longer a labor of love, but a drudgery in which I had no interest," recalled Hill. "One day I put on my hat and coat, walked out of the place without saying good-bye, and made Mr. Williams a present of the other half of my cherished brain child."

Williams would keep the magazine alive for another eleven years but, according to Hill, he fired Igoe shortly after Napoleon's departure. Several years later Williams remarked to Stephen Austin Weir, one of Hill's closest confidants, "When Napoleon Hill walked out of my life something that can never be replaced went with him." And, as a final irony, many years later Napoleon encountered Igoe on the streets of Nashville, Tennessee. He described the meeting this way:

"Just ahead of me I saw a queer looking creature, weighing approximately 300 pounds, wearing a stovepipe hat, a dress suit two sizes too large, with his hair hanging down to his shoulders. When I caught up with him I was astonished to see that it was my former employee. He had memorized, verbatim, some lessons on Applied Psychology I had written and published in the *Golden Rule,* and was then 'lecturing' in Nashville, as a full-fledged, expert psychologist."

★ ★ ★

Napoleon Hill was a man who had already absorbed a life-time's worth of crushing defeats and setbacks, and would absorb that many more in the rest of his life. But none of them affected him as deeply and as personally as losing his first magazine. On one level, it was like losing his own child: *Hill's Golden Rule* had been an extension of him—his talent, his philosophy, his passion. On another level, he had failed again. The security his wife and children so desperately needed had slipped away once more, even as it hovered so near he could touch it.

In Lumberport, Florence and the boys girded themselves for another long, threadbare winter living off her family's charity. Years later, David Hill would recall, "I grew up as a poor relative of the richest family in town. . . . Most of the time, all [Florence] lived on was faith and hope things would turn better for her."

In Chicago, Napoleon grieved. His courage and faith abandoned him. His love for humanity gave way to bitterness and cynicism. For the first time in his life, he was unable to focus on a goal. For the first time in his life, he took no action, made no move to start climbing the mountain again. He became immersed in self-pity and immobilized by it.

Hill's paralysis lasted more than a month and might well have consumed him completely but for the actions of his former associates. Unannounced and completely unexpected, a piece of mail came to him one day. It was from Williams, and it contained a certificate of deposit for twenty-five thousand dollars made out to Hill. Napoleon was stunned and then elated at the sight of so much money—not because of the relief from financial burdens it offered, but because it was enough to start another magazine. Nap's entrepreneurial juices were flowing again. He was ready to climb another mountain.

But there were strings attached to the money. Reading

closer, Hill discovered that, by cashing the check, he would release his claims on and participation in *Golden Rule*. Napoleon would later claim that this stipulation alone caused him to reject the settlement, that it would have meant turning his back on all that he had been preaching and trading his principles for a bag of gold. This may indeed have been the case, but the provisions of the buyout probably also contained a much more serious threat to Napoleon's principles and goals: In a transaction of this type, the buyout contract would typically include language barring the selling party—in this case, Hill—from becoming involved with a competing publication for a period of years.

Whatever the cause, Hill returned the money and declined the offer. But the seed was planted. He was mobilized again. He had suddenly conceived another "definite chief aim" in life: He would start another magazine. If it was worth twenty-five thousand dollars to Williams for Hill *not* to publish, he could find investors who would put up that much *to help him* publish.

At roughly the same time, the October 1920 issue of *Golden Rule* came out, and Napoleon had added motivation for making his new enterprise succeed. Not only had his name been dropped from the magazine's logo and masthead, but a page-two editorial by G. B. Williams informed readers that, due to criticism of Napoleon's editorial policy, it had been necessary to "eradicate" him. Seething with fury over this final act of humiliation and betrayal, Hill became a man possessed, descending on each obstacle to his start-up like a whirlwind and turning it to dust.

By early 1921, he had done it again. He had moved to New York, raised seed money from friends, found a printer, designed the new format, hired a trusted associate editor, and written all the articles and most of the ads for the first issue. In April 1921, the first issue of *Napoleon Hill's Magazine* hit the newsstands with an impact that sent vibrations shaking through America's self-help press.

The April cover left no doubt about Hill's mood. It was dominated by an announcement in large bold type:

> A National Monthly Magazine about human beings, by human beings, for human beings, "With charity for all and malice toward none," edited on the *real* Golden Rule basis, taking up the work where it was discontinued in *Hill's Golden Rule*. No chain of gold is tied around our pen.

The cover also included a prominent "Editor's Creed" that pledged to help people "see the necessity of placing principle above the dollar and humanity above the selfish individual whose only object in life is to get without giving."

Even in his rage, Hill was a masterful promoter. He needed to create the immediate perception among readers and advertisers that *Napoleon Hill's Magazine* was a publication of major significance. Thus, he chose an eight- by eleven-inch trim size for the new magazine—an inch taller and an inch wider than *Golden Rule*. Sitting side by side on newsstands, the difference in size was striking: *Napoleon Hill's Magazine* was twenty percent larger than its main competitor. His big magazine cost twenty-five cents a copy, while the diminutive *Golden Rule* commanded but twenty cents. And at the bottom of the cover, in bigger, bolder type than anything but the logo, he ran the legend, 100,000 CIRCULATION. In much smaller type beneath this guarantee, he added, BY DECEMBER THIRTY FIRST 1921.

Inside, Napoleon got immediately to the business of settling scores. On the first body page of the first issue, he launched a three-page editorial entitled, "An Indictment Without Malice! Facts Concerning *Hill's Golden Rule.*" It was an extraordinarily persuasive rebuttal to the broadside he had suffered from *Golden Rule*.

He began by taking readers back to the inception of *Hill's Golden Rule,* to the bright passions that poured forth as the evil specter of the war was erased, to the meditation that produced "a little brown covered magazine" dedicated to service, truth, and beauty, the cornerstones of civilization. He wrote of the effect a magazine based on the Golden Rule had on people:

> During the year 1920 I went over the United States on a speaking tour, and the wild enthusiasm with which the people received me . . . the courtesies which they extended me told me in most unmistakable terms that my message, through *Hill's Golden Rule* had struck very deeply in their hearts. . . . As I came into contact with hundreds of thousands of the people of America . . . Catholics and Protestants, Jews and Gentiles, Republicans and Democrats and Socialists, all races and creeds . . . they all received me with open arms as being of their kind, and I knew I had been giving people, through my magazine, that for which they were thirsty: A kindly and friendly philosophy, a visualization of our common 'one-ness'.

And then he told how mean-spirited people "who profit from the control of . . . the common people" had perverted Williams's honorable instincts, forcing him to "break his contract with me without the formality or courtesy of ever talking the matter over. . . ."

Hill explained the duplicity of Williams's "eradication" editorial and told of receiving hundreds of letters from readers expressing shock and indignation over his removal. He printed one sample from an Iowan named Earl Ticen who complained that the new *Golden Rule* "is simply paper, ink and hired men."

"From all over the country," wrote Hill, "subscribers have canceled, many of them demanding the return of their money on the grounds they bought one thing and are receiving another, and gradually the magazine is disappearing from the newsstands." There was a lesson in this, Hill sermonized: "The wages of sin is death. No success or fortune that is not built on truth and justice can endure."

But *Napoleon Hill's Magazine* was conceived as a platform for the pursuit of nobler things than vengeance, and even the first issue got quickly on to the higher calling of spreading the gospel of the Golden Rule. Napoleon's more virtuous instincts were stimulated by his new associate editor, an engineer he had met in the Texas oil fields named Stephen Austin Weir. Weir not only brought some relief to Napoleon's workload but also became a lifelong confidant and perhaps Hill's closest friend. Many years later, Hill wrote of Weir, "He came into my life at a time when I was hot-headed, flighty, and perhaps a bit too inclined to take myself seriously.

"To him, more than any other, do I owe the seasoning process that has stripped me of the weakness of vanity, the vulgarity of egotism, the mistake of feeling self-important."

Napoleon Hill's Magazine had the same basic editorial concept as *Golden Rule,* but there were significant differences between the two. Napoleon himself was still the star attraction and poured thousands of words of advice and philosophy into each issue. But the new magazine featured more articles written by outside contributors, who ranged from successful businesspeople to physicians and psychologists. With the outside contributors came a heavy diet of service features. Each issue contained a selection of how-to articles providing readers advice on things like selling one's self, getting a better job, concentrating, and building self-confidence.

In addition, each issue was sprinkled with one-page inspirational messages presented in a large-type layout that was, literally, suitable for framing. These "page essays" did for *Napoleon Hill's Magazine* what display advertisements did for other magazines—they provided a change of graphic and editorial pace between articles and opinion pieces. Their focus ranged from Lincoln's Gettysburg Address to Hill's own sermons on subjects like "Golden Rule Thoughts," "Intolerance," and "Alone With My Conscience." A full-page ad headlined, "You Need These Beautiful Wall-Hangers to Advertise Your Business" offered readers the opportunity to purchase mounted, posterlike displays of their favorite essay—with the name of their own business printed below—for "much less than 25 cents [each] in lots of 1,000 and upward." The idea was for the buyer to distribute the ads to his or her customers as a promotion that would yield two benefits. "In giving away these hangers," read the ad, "you are doing more than advertising your business or profession—you are PLANTING CONSTRUCTIVE THOUGHTS WHERE THEY WILL HELP MAKE THIS A BETTER WORLD."

Such modest enterprises were an important source of revenue, however small, for the cash-strapped magazine. It was, if anything, more of a shoestring operation than *Golden Rule* had been, and it attracted very little advertising—perhaps because its high-minded editor and publisher did not want the distraction. In any event, each issue of *Napoleon Hill's Magazine* contained a variety of house ads for cash-generating businesses. Subscription promotions touted featured authors like Harriet Luella McCollum, who wrote about applied psychology and whose gender gave Hill a promotional entrée to wave at working women. Another subscription promotion promised a free six-month scholarship to any business college for the person who sold the most *Napoleon Hill's Magazine* subscriptions each month. Other ads hawked photos of a statue of Abraham Lincoln, membership in the Peptomists Club (for devotees of applied psychology—*NHM* was its "official organ"), and the Co-Operative Club, a social organization that gave readers of *NHM* the opportunity to meet at local places, make valuable business contacts, and find "happiness through constructive service."

With grit, creativity, and sheer personal will, Napoleon achieved a remarkable milestone in 1921: He turned a profit on his start-up magazine in its first year of existence. Then, as now, such accomplishments were extraordinarily rare. Poorly capitalized ventures like Nap's almost inevitably failed without ever showing a profit, and even well-capitalized start-ups typically operated in red ink for several years.

While he lacked capital and publishing sophistication, Hill had a vast popular following on which to build. It was his own "Law of Increasing Returns" played out in real life: He had put his heart and soul into *Golden Rule* and his promotional lectures—he had done more than he was paid for—and the equity he had earned in his former pursuits was now being invested in his new magazine.

Hill's peripatetic pace of lectures, speeches, and personal appearances began anew by the summer of 1921. Stimulated by ads in the magazine informing the public of his availability for "a limited number of engagements," he spoke to people in sales and advertising, to business groups, and to civic clubs and colleges. But unlike his early days with *Golden Rule,* when he traveled anywhere to speak anytime for nothing more than the opportunity to promote his magazine and his philosophy, now he was commanding a fee of one hundred dollars or more plus expenses. In a letter to Florence dated May 29, he celebrated his first fee, commenting, "Last year I was glad to go anywhere for my traveling expenses, and a year before that I would have gone at the drop of a hat and paid my own expenses. Slowly but surely we are arriving."

By this time, Napoleon probably enjoyed public speaking even more than writing because it gave him the chance to see how his words and visions could move people, to feel the crackling emotions he aroused in them, and to receive directly the praise and adulation that his audiences bestowed on him. It was during this period that Hill began billing himself as "the Billy Sunday of business evangelism," after the famous fundamentalist preacher who had spread biblical gospel with fiery street-corner sermons throughout America.

The appellation fit—for Hill the writer and Hill the speaker. His articles and speeches were liberally sprinkled with biblical proverbs, and he himself became a prolific source of original quotations that were often eloquent and sometimes profound. "The most unhappy mortals on earth," he told his audience, "are those who receive nothing for their services except wages."

To help people cope with one of their six basic fears— the fear of criticism—he offered, "We want to hear the truth about ourselves, but woe be unto the one who hands it to us without a sugar coating."

And to provide current-day proof of his Law of Compensation, he created this one-liner about an American political activist who emigrated to the Soviet Union: "Emma Goldman is said to be lonesome and dissatisfied with her environment in Russia, which only goes to show that when we get that which we try to impose on others we squeal like stuck pigs."

Every issue of the magazine, every speech he made, and every conversation he joined inevitably produced a torrent of these homilies.

His public speaking services during this period were based on two lecture series. The Magic Ladder of Success, geared to business groups, covered the fifteen principles on which Napoleon believed success was based. True to his Golden Rule philosophy, Napoleon wove into this presentation his most cherished humanistic ideals: friendly cooperation and the elimination of racial and religious intolerance, hatred, and envy.

His other lecture series, The End of the Rainbow, was a purely inspirational narrative oriented to civic and religious groups. It was based on what Hill called "the seven major turning points in my life." He told stories of his professional and personal triumphs and failures and the lessons he had learned from both . . . lessons that he passed on to others in hopes of helping them through their own lives.

Hill's incredibly persuasive speaking style soon led to an innovation in modern communications. Because the magazine was doing so well, he decided, in 1921, to create and distribute a mail-order instruction course called The Science of Success. To take advantage of Napoleon's near-hypnotic speaking style, the offering included not only ten printed lessons but six phonograph records as well. One could now read *and* listen to Napoleon Hill. This pioneering blend of communications vehicles was an early forerunner of motivational audio programs, a specialized media that would eventually become a multimillion-dollar industry in its own right.

Inevitably, the great casualty of Napoleon Hill's devotion to inspiring success and goodness in America was his participation in his own family life. He and Florence still exchanged letters nearly every day, but they saw each other only in brief snatches of time, usually in cities where Nap was lecturing. His personal contact with the children was even less frequent—once or twice a year when he could get to Lumberport or they could all meet at his parents' home in Wise. Indeed, Jimmie and Blair, desperate for a more secure family environment, had been sent to live with their grandparents in Wise. Gradually, the passions that marked Napoleon's letters to Florence in the previous decade were displaced by attempts to rally her sagging morale and overcome the spiritual distance that was beginning to separate them.

Late that year, a pattern was beginning to emerge: After years of struggling alone to solve family and financial problems, Florence was reaching a point where she did not even bother to mention the problems to Nap. One such incident occurred in October when Florence became very ill—a fact she didn't mention to Napoleon until she had to explain why she couldn't join him in New York. Upon hearing this, Napoleon wrote, "Dear, I had no idea you were very sick, or else I would have been there with you. I naturally concluded that as long as you were able to write me every day you could not be very sick.

"You must come out of it because I need you up here with me to help me do some window shopping every night along Fifth Avenue and Broadway and these other beautiful streets. I do hope it will not be two weeks before you can come."

The rest of the letter was filled with cheerful images of the sumptuous pleasures and comforts that awaited her upon her arrival in New York. Like a die crafted to cast the same form a thousand times in perfect repetition, the elements of this letter would appear and reappear with only superficial variations through most of the remainder of their married life . . . Napoleon's eloquent apology for past or recent shortcomings, followed by descriptions of the good life that awaited just around the corner.

Florence's feelings of emotional separation from Napoleon were undoubtedly exacerbated by the contrast in their lifestyles. Nap faithfully sent her checks when he had income, but his support was diminished by the liberal allowance he took to maintain the standard of living he thought appropriate to a public figure like himself. While his family lived modestly—at best—Nap lived in nice hotels, entertained in popular restaurants, and maintained a wardrobe of fine suits. In fairness to Napoleon, he had to project a public image of accomplishment to have credibility as a business evangelist and expert on success, but the panache with which he carried off this appearance, and the contrast it created between his and his family's lives, would nourish the seeds of doubt about his competence and devotion that were sprouting at home.

While Napoleon's domestic life began to erode, his career entered 1922 with more momentum than ever before. His magazine was already the envy of small publishers across the country; his bold cover legend that just a few months earlier had promised a circulation of one hundred thousand by the end of 1921 now promised a circulation of three hundred thousand by the end of 1922. Demand for his lectures—even with a $150 fee—far exceeded the time he could devote to them. And his work on the Carnegie project flourished as his personal fame easily opened doors to America's richest and most famous business figures.

Ironically, at the height of his personal stature and fame, it was a letter from a prison inmate that led to the next great turn in Hill's life, one that set him on the career path that would produce America's first comprehensive philosophy of success.

The letter was written by Butler R. Storke, a convicted forger serving a two-year sentence in the Ohio State Penitentiary. Storke was a college graduate and had served with distinction in World War I, achieving the rank of captain in the field artillery. He had not denied his guilt nor made excuses for his crime when he went to prison. Instead, he had volunteered to improve the prison's depleted library.

Since the prison had no budget for acquiring books, Storke organized a letter-writing campaign, asking publishers throughout the country to donate books to the prison so that the library might offer inmates the kind of information, ideas, and inspiration that would help them lead successful, constructive lives.

Storke's appeal was a great success. Books and magazines and even correspondence courses poured into the institution, among them *Napoleon Hill's Magazine* and Hill's Science of Success home-study program.

In his letter to Napoleon, Storke said he had read every issue of the magazine and suggested that Hill's success philosophy, his words of faith and encouragement, and his advice and leadership could be a tremendous help in educating and rehabilitating criminals such as himself. He asked Hill to work with him to perfect an idea he had for a correspondence course tailored to prison inmates.

Nap seized the opportunity without a moment's hesitation. It was wildly unorthodox—prisons were for punishment, not rehabilitation, in 1922. And it was a chance to literally save men's souls, the highest possible calling for any evangelist, be his orientation biblical or business. With his customary élan and reckless enthusiasm, Napoleon plunged into the project.

Hill visited the prison to inspect Storke's Intra-Wall Home Study system and became even more enthusiastic about "the practical and beneficial service he was rendering." Even as he offered Storke suggestions and logistical support, Napoleon was going one step further, once again setting aside "selfish prudence" to take a risk that few people would have even considered. "I began immediately to bring about his freedom," recalled Napoleon, "so he might carry on his work under more favorable conditions."

Never one for half-measures, Napoleon pleaded Storke's case to everyone from the prison warden to Ohio's governor—and won. The key to Napoleon's effectiveness was his creation of a company—the Intra-Wall Institute—that would perfect and popularize the course. "I had organized a legally constituted educational institution with the object of not only intensifying the educational system my protégé had begun, but with the intention of extending the system to all other prisons throughout the country," recalled Hill. With a formal plan and his own good name on the line, Napoleon swayed the governor. On August 14, 1922, Butler Storke walked out of prison and into Napoleon Hill's employment, drawing a salary of $250 a month. Hill's promotional instincts were released full force on the event.

"The day he left the penitentiary I had the representatives of the press on hand to write the story of the purpose of his release, and the newsreel representatives were also on hand to make news pictures of the story," wrote Hill. "The next day and for more than a month thereafter, the story was given space in practically every newspaper in the country, some of them giving front page, full column space with runner headlines."

Perhaps nothing better illustrates the strengths and weaknesses of Hill at this time in his life than his thoughts as he met Storke at the prison gate. Completely ignoring the fact that he was gambling his own stature and prestige on the conduct of a convicted forger, Hill's mind was completely focused on the incredible opportunity for success Storke now had—primarily because he had failed so completely before. "I hope you realize that, despite having the stain of prison on you, the opportunity which has been dumped into your lap has given you a better start in life than you had the day you graduated from college," Hill told Storke.

Years later, Napoleon would use that incident as an anecdote to explain one of his principles of success. "The world was his oyster, merely for the taking," explained Hill. "Everyone who saw him volunteered aid. The world is like that when a man happens by chance, or by choice, to relate himself to other people in the proper manner."

As it happened, Storke encouraged Napoleon's confidence. He applied his full energies and intellect to the Intra-Wall Home Study course and within a year had put the finishing touches on one of the era's most provocative and promising concepts in penal reform. Storke did not work alone. Despite his magazines, lectures, and Carnegie-project research, Napoleon was intensely involved in the creation of the course and materials, and especially in organizing and running the business. He got seed money for books, materials, and office expenses from Ralph Weeks, a longtime contact who was the president of the International Correspondence Schools. He then raised money from private contributors to fund promotion of the course to other penal institutions and communities.

Hill also conceived a unique marketing plan, one so clever as to suggest the work of an inspired genius.

"The plan was very simple," wrote Hill. "It consisted of my making a complete personal character analysis of every inmate of the prison with the aid of a questionnaire I had used in the organization of my philosophy, after which the various members of our staff delivered speeches before Rotary clubs, chambers of commerce, churches and other places, and 'sold' prisoners to the members of the audience. By this I mean we induced people to look over the records of a hundred or more prisoners, as indicated by the questionnaires they had filled out, and to pick out one or more men whom they would sponsor from that time forward, and for whom they paid a flat fee of $50 per man [for] education.

"In the little town of Shelby, Ohio, where I first tried the plan, the members of the local chamber of commerce bought 16 prisoners and paid us $800."

Hill and Storke had simply sought a way to generate enough cash from their good works to perpetuate their not-for-profit organization. Hill's plan filled that requirement very well. Too well, in fact, for the plan had the unmistakable potential to generate far greater quantities of cash than the modest amounts sought by its idealistic creators. That potential quickly corrupted two of the institution's directors and, through them, the institution itself.

Though Napoleon would blame himself for a lack of caution in selecting the Intra-Wall Institute's directors, his choices seemed to be in harmony with the humanitarian intent of the project. Along with himself, he chose the chaplain of the prison in which Storke had started work on the course, who had supported and aided Storke's work. The third director was a close friend of the chaplain. Alas, the man of God and his friend turned out to be men of straw when the potential for big money passed under their noses. The two directors wanted to use the Institute to get rich. Their greed and aggressiveness offended and angered Hill.

"The school had hardly begun to function when it became obvious that it was to be converted into a political racket of the meanest sort," Hill recalled. "Therefore, I quietly wrote Ralph Weeks . . . giving him a detailed statement of what had happened to my project, folded my own tent and returned to New York. Mr. Weeks shut off the monthly expense account and the two politicians took over what was left of the school. Shortly thereafter my protégé became again entangled with the law and was sent back to prison."

But that was not the end of it for Napoleon. The Intra-Wall Institute debacle came to a head late in 1923, and its aftermath wiped out Hill in a matter of months. The main players in his demise were the two embittered Intra-Wall directors and Hill's old *Specialty Salesman* nemesis, Bob Hicks.

According to Napoleon, Hicks's personal vendetta did not end with Napoleon's departure from *Golden Rule*. If anything, Hicks's hatred grew exponentially as Hill had risen from the ashes to create an even greater success with *Napoleon Hill's Magazine* and to spread his personal reputation and stature as America's resident philosopher-laureate of success and ethics.

One way or another, Hicks tapped into the messy climax of the Intra-Wall project and found in Nap's estranged directors two angry men who were ready to participate wholeheartedly in any campaign that would inflict damage on Hill. Hicks used them and their accounts of the Intra-Wall

Institute affair to set in motion a deadly efficient all-out attack on Napoleon.

First, Hicks launched a scathing attack on Hill's character in *Specialty Salesman,* based on the accusations of the Intra-Wall directors. Concurrently, he hired thugs to disrupt Hill's public lectures by shouting accusations and challenging his integrity. Once again, Hill was hopelessly trapped. His only effective recourse would have been to destroy Hicks's credibility by slinging his own mud. This, however, would have been a complete violation of his Golden Rule principles—a denial of everything he stood for. So he attempted to ignore the accusations in hopes that his own stature and reputation would be enough to ride out the storm.

Indeed, he might well have ridden out this storm but for the fact that he was, as ever, financially vulnerable. The public furor Hicks created took an immediate toll on the cash flow of *Napoleon Hill's Magazine,* scaring off advertisers, cutting into subscription and newsstand sales, and reducing revenues from the magazine's various house-ad promotions to a trickle. Quickly, the magazine fell behind in payments to its printer, and Hicks delivered his masterstroke: He offered to buy the printer's mortgage on *Napoleon Hill's Magazine.* However bullish the printer might have felt about the magazine's chances of recovering from this sudden setback, Hicks's offer was an opportunity to eliminate his own financial risk completely. The printer sold. When Hill failed to make good on his payments due, Hicks ruthlessly foreclosed and immediately stopped publication of the magazine.

For good measure, Hicks launched one final act in his personal crusade to destroy Napoleon: He convinced the U.S. Post Office to investigate Hill for mail fraud, apparently in connection with either his subscription promotions or a 1923 house-ad campaign selling shares in the Hill Publishing Trust, the company Napoleon formed to publish the magazine and his home-study books and records. In any event, there were no grounds for fraud. There had been no violations of the law, and the only act of bad faith in the entire mess had been perpetrated by Hicks himself. The postal investigation exonerated Napoleon completely, but he could take no satisfaction in that. The damage had already been done. At age forty, for the second time in three years, Napoleon Hill walked forth a pauper. Everything he owned had been lost in the mayhem that resulted from the Intra-Wall Institute scandal.

The bleak irony of Hill's demise was the fact that few enterprises in the 1920s could have been more idealistic or humanitarian in concept than *Napoleon Hill's Magazine* and the Intra-Wall Institute, yet in seeking to stir goodness in men's souls these enterprises had stirred mean-spirited men to a blood lust that destroyed everything. As the victim of this irony, Napoleon might reasonably have seen the entire conflict as a struggle between good and evil, with the outcome as proof that the struggle for good is doomed to failure.

And perhaps he did consider this interpretation and others that might justify a more callous and miserly approach to life. But in the end, his belief in his own gospel won out. His failure, he wrote, stemmed not from the forces of evil but from his own human errors:

> The truth is this: My lack of caution in relating myself to others had resulted in my drifting into difficulties. Reasonable precautionary methods such as Carnegie or Henry Ford would surely have employed if they had been in my place would have saved me all that trouble, to say nothing of saving my property and the money put into my magazine by my friends. I hold no brief for myself and offer no alibis. I failed because I richly deserved to fail, but I do have the satisfaction of being able to say truthfully that my failure was not without its appropriate compensa-

tion in the form of the changes it forced me to make in
my method of relating myself to others thereafter.

There was one final blow to his spirit to come from this
dark period. When he returned to Chicago to gather his
few possessions and get on with the next chapter in his life,
he found the building in which he had stored his goods had
burned to the ground, destroying everything in it. In terms
of material value, Napoleon's losses were minimal. His
emotional and professional losses, however, were staggering.
Gone were dozens of letters and notes from Woodrow
Wilson, including his approval of a Hill proposal that the
president used to sell war bonds. Gone were the autographed
pictures of Wilson, Bell, and others. Gone was President
Taft's letter endorsing Hill for employment. Gone was a series
of letters from Manuel L. Quezon, who corresponded
with Hill prior to becoming president of the Philippine
Commonwealth.

And, most devastating of all, gone were Hill's bulging files
of confidential questionnaires completed by such luminaries
as Luther Burbank, Thomas Edison, and hundreds more who
participated in his research on the philosophy of success.

Many years later, Napoleon still recalled the feelings of
horror and dismay that swept through him as he viewed the
charred carnage of the building: "The loss of my magazine
cost all the money I had . . . my confidence in men had been
shaken terribly . . . but those losses were as nothing compared
to the destruction of things that could never be restored;
things associated with the memories of men who had been
my greatest benefactors at a time in my life when their recognition was about the only real asset I possessed.

"But I pulled myself together . . . Then and there I
reached the conclusion I would never again attach so much
importance to any material thing."

★ ★ ★

Napoleon Hill had all the human weaknesses he confessed to and maybe more. But whatever else might be said of him, nobody bounced back from adversity better.

Borrowing one thousand dollars to cover his living expenses until he could get started again, Hill boarded a train for Ohio. He had no specific prospects there, just the belief that "the place one loses something of value is an appropriate place to go back and search for it."

Applying his own principles of success to the situation, Hill quickly set a definite main purpose for himself. He would purchase and operate a business college—a truly immodest goal for one so recently bankrupted, since he calculated the cost of such a purchase at one hundred thousand dollars or more. As ever, the challenge brought out the best in Napoleon.

He began by systematically reviewing cities and locations that met his criteria, then focusing on specific properties. He found what he wanted in the Metropolitan Business College on the west side of Cleveland. The school was housed in a newly constructed building and its private owner would sell for $125,000. The purchase price was, of course, a problem, but Hill solved that by conceiving a creative plan that gave everyone involved an opportunity to profit without taking undue risks.

In essence, Hill's financial plan was a quasi rental-purchase arrangement. He would operate the school on a three-year contract following a business plan he and the owner mutually endorsed. The contract gave him the option to purchase the school for cash at any time, or to turn it back to the owner. Until Hill purchased the school, the owner would receive nominal rental payments as well as a share of the net profits.

The school's owner jumped on the deal, primarily because of Hill's astute business plan. He intended to dramatically increase the school's enrollment through a variety of promotional activities, the most important being weekly lectures on Hill's philosophy of achievement for graduating seniors in all high schools within a fifty-mile radius of the college.

Leaving day-to-day administrative matters in the hands of a carefully chosen, reliable financial expert, Hill began stumping for his new enterprise early in 1924—three lectures a day, five days a week. The results were predictable. Just as surely as he had inspired hope, action, and purpose in adult audiences for years, he stirred the passions of area teenagers to take control of their lives, to set their own goals without deference to the limitations others would put on them, and to satisfy their ambitions in ways that would help others achieve the same satisfaction. By autumn, enrollment in the Metropolitan College of Business had reached full capacity.

In short order, Hill added practical courses in journalism, salesmanship, advertising, and public speaking to the curriculum, and trained other members of Metropolitan's staff to deliver the high school lectures so that he could free up time to get back on the lecture circuit. One of these engagements found him delivering the commencement address at Salem College in West Virginia. This appearance would have great repercussions later in his life, for it was at this gathering that he met Jennings Randolph, a man who would be elected to the House of Representatives in 1932 and would eventually become an intimate of President Franklin D. Roosevelt.

Despite his remarkable success at rebuilding the college's enrollment, these were difficult years for Hill and his family. As in any new business start-up, personal income was strictly limited during the time it took to establish a positive cash flow and a healthy operating profit. That meant more months of hand-to-mouth struggle for Florence and the boys, and still more long periods of separation. Napoleon tried to ease the financial pain by selling editorials and articles to a variety of publications, and with his public speaking activities, but there was never enough to provide real comfort and security for his family.

Florence began to lose hope. By 1925, Napoleon's letters to her signaled a marriage at the crisis point. He pleaded with her to write. He painted fanciful visions of vacations, presents, the home they would buy next year based on how well things were now shaping up. He urged her to shake off her depression by buying a new outfit or bobbing her hair. And, in letter after letter, he expressed his own haunting loneliness and doubt.

In the dead of winter, 1925, Napoleon hit bottom. He wrote to Florence, "You have no idea what it is like when not a soul on earth encourages you, and all the negative forces pour in on you. It takes superhuman strength of will to throw them off. I would give anything if I had someone, even though they did not mean it or believe it, to tell me they KNEW I COULD SUCCEED.

"I would like to hear this every day and sometimes twice a day.

"I keep telling myself this . . . but that other self in me keeps denying it when I say it."

Later that year, with more cash coming from the college, more paid public-speaking engagements, and the launch of a promising new enterprise—the Thirteen Club, patterned after the Co-Operative Club from his *Napoleon Hill's Magazine* days—Florence's spirits recovered somewhat, and Napoleon began to burst with optimism again. In a letter dated July 13, 1925, he promised Florence and the boys that they would soon be buying a house, a car, and a pony. Unlike earlier letters in which such visions were expressed as the vague hopes of a burdened man, this was written by a confident, ebullient Napoleon who could now purvey his recent past without shame:

"I have stood by the Law of Success lecture and my 15 points for more than seven years. At times they only seemed to mock me, when I was talking of success to others while my own family suffered for the necessities. I have not known just why I did this. At times I wondered, as you have done, if I would not have been better off to have forgotten it all and have gone back to some little job as a bookkeeper, where I could have earned at least a modest living. BUT there was something that would not let me do it."

He finished the letter with a poignant epitaph that summarized both the heroic strengths and the ignoble weaknesses of his being.

"I have stood my grounds, suffered, been disappointed, and given disappointment to others," he wrote, "all because I could not do otherwise. I was simply helpless in the matter . . . I would have changed my course a dozen times in the past six or seven years IF I COULD HAVE DONE SO."

It was perhaps the only time in Hill's life that he would concede that there is a part of one's destiny that is out of one's control.

And it was ever thus for Napoleon. His driving force required a stage much larger than the Metropolitan Business College, and audiences much vaster than classrooms and civic clubs. Even as the college prospered and demand for his speeches in the Cleveland area expanded, Napoleon was being tugged into yet another adventure.

It began when he got involved in the political campaign of a man who had befriended him over the years. Crisscrossing the state to stump for the candidate, he spoke one evening to a Canton business group whose numbers included Don Mellet, publisher of the *Canton Daily News.* Mellet was impressed with Hill's fire-and-brimstone approach to politics, education, and achievement, and he was fascinated by Hill's lifelong dedication to researching the principles of success and failure. Before parting company, the two men agreed that Napoleon would return to Canton after the campaign to deliver a series of lectures on his philosophy of achievement under the sponsorship of the newspaper.

Early in 1926, the relationship between Hill and Mellet had grown into a living example of the Master Mind Alliance Hill had adopted from Carnegie. Along with a high-profile newspaper advertising campaign for Hill's lectures, Mellet planned for Hill to write a daily column that he would publish in his own paper and syndicate to newspapers across the country. The syndication effort was backed by a unique incentive: Newspapers picking up the column could call on Napoleon himself to deliver a six-lesson course in salesmanship for their best advertisers.

They tested the idea in Canton and surrounding cities with excellent results. Napoleon impulsively assigned his interest in the college to the financial administrator and entered into a partnership with Mellet.

Mellet was an aggressive, thick-skinned newspaperman, and a strict taskmaster who bullied and bullied Napoleon to achieve ever higher journalistic standards. Given Nap's penchant for sharp-tongued arrogance and his rightful pride in the power of his own writing, the two men's relationship probably should have exploded almost instantly into enmity. It didn't. Buoyed by a strong mutual respect, each accepted in the other man his unique style and, together, they got the syndicated column off to an excellent start.

As soon as the syndicated column was established, the two men turned their entrepreneurial focus to the biggest prize of all: Mellet wanted Hill to turn his lifetime of research on the principles of success into a book. Actually, it would be an eight-volume set of books—the grandest, most complete treatise on success ever written. Mellet was so enthused he told Hill he would resign his post at the newspaper to devote full time to the success of the "success" book.

While Napoleon toiled to organize and write the massive

text, Mellet pieced together a plan to raise the fifty thousand dollars they needed to print and promote the books.

Just as Mellet was closing in on the financing they needed, both men got caught up in a tense subplot. Mellet's reporters found evidence that Prohibition gangsters were selling narcotics and bootleg liquor to Canton schoolchildren and had bribed members of the local police force to look the other way. This knowledge infuriated both men. Mellet launched an outraged exposé in the *Daily News*. Hill used his contacts with Ohio governor Vic Donahey to bring about a state investigation of Canton's corrupt police department, then took over the day-to-day management of a team of private investigators hired by the *Daily News* to conduct an independent probe.

It was a noble but lonely cause. According to Hill, Canton's movers and shakers were thoroughly intimidated by the gangsters. The other newspaper in Canton ignored the story, and even the city's religious leaders refused Hill's call to action.

As the furor over police corruption settled into methodical investigation by state authorities, Mellet was finally able to complete arrangements for the financing of their book project. He had convinced Judge Elbert H. Gary, chairman of the board of U.S. Steel, to underwrite the project with a guaranteed purchase of copies for every management employee of the giant firm. Hill and Mellet estimated that the U.S. Steel order would be worth $150,000—and Gary offered to help them create inducements that would help them win similar orders from other corporate giants. Mellet and Gary set a date in late July 1926 to work through the details and create a contract.

A week before the scheduled meeting, as Mellet came home from work a gangster and one of the renegade police officers were waiting for him in ambush. As Mellet emerged from his garage, his assassins sprayed him with a vicious hail of machine-gun fire, killing him instantly.

Hill escaped a similar fate only because car trouble had delayed his return to Canton until the next morning. As soon as he arrived home he learned of Mellet's brutal murder, then received an anonymous phone call telling him he had one hour to get out of town. Realizing the situation was hopeless, Hill left immediately, not even pausing to pack.

Once more, he had struggled and scratched to follow the course of a rainbow. Once more, he had come within an arm's length of the promised pot of gold. And once more, it had been snatched from him just as he reached to touch it. Napoleon Hill would spend the forty-third year of his life in hiding in West Virginia, destitute, unable to support his stunned family, unwilling to go out of doors without a pistol in his pocket. For the first time in his life, he experienced the pain of constant fear.

CHAPTER 5

1927-1933

At first, life went on for Napoleon. In a letter from an unspecified location to Florence dated July 19, 1926, a few days after Mellet's murder, he suggested he had returned to Canton to try to start over. "We have all been so torn up on account of Mr. Mellet's death that we have done but little work," he wrote. "I am just now getting down to business again, as the enclosed advertisement will show."

In the same letter he invited Florence to join him in Canton for a Sunday picnic.

A month later, in another letter to Florence, he outlined an ambitious fall speaking campaign in Indiana. The enthusiasm and the grandeur of the plan were vintage Napoleon Hill: six months of lectures, overwhelming publicity, and active support "from the entire political machinery of Indiana," including personal participation by the governor. The tour would start in Indianapolis where he would have the backing of all three newspapers, share the podium with the mayor and the chief of police, make his entrance to the rousing accompaniment of the police department marching band, and receive the support of the state's most potent sociopolitical force—the Ku Klux Klan.

"It is the most elaborately planned lecture ever put on in that state," he gushed. But there were dark shadows on Napoleon's life as he wrote that letter in September. Indeed, it was the last letter from Napoleon that Florence would keep for more than a year, for the same hoods that gunned down Mellet were stalking Napoleon.

Hill received his first death threat shortly after Mellet's murder. It was delivered over the phone by the renegade cop who had slaughtered Mellet. The message was short and sweet: Get out of Canton or suffer Mellet's fate.

Nap had no choice in the matter. Despite his feisty temperament and his own lethal marksmanship with pistols and rifles, he was not a killer and could not hope to win the Canton war. There were simply too many gangsters, and they had too many ties to the local police, politicians, and judges. Napoleon left town almost immediately.

His first stop was Cleveland, where he tried to salvage the lecture tours he and Mellet had been planning. The lectures had immediate priority over the manuscript because he needed cash desperately. His letter to Florence regarding the Indiana tour was written from Cleveland.

But Mellet's murderers had no intention of letting Hill live that close to Canton. They kept the pressure on and shortly after his letter to Florence, Napoleon disappeared from Ohio under the cover of night. He drove deep into the mountains of West Virginia to hide out at the home of relatives. His exile would last a year. It was a year of private purgatory for Hill, a year spent in the grip of terror, motionless and unproductive.

"During the time I was in hiding," Hill wrote in his memoirs, "I seldom left the house at night, and when I did step out I kept my hand on an automatic pistol, ready for immediate action. If a strange automobile stopped in front of the house I went into the basement and carefully scrutinized its occupants, through the basement windows . . . I was so subdued by fear of assassination that I kept a body guard near me day and night. . . ."

And so it was that Napoleon Hill spent October 26, 1926—his forty-third birthday—in hiding. And he would remain in hiding for nearly all of 1927. While other men his age enjoyed the plentiful bounty of America's ever burgeoning richness and the manic pleasures of the final years of the Roaring Twenties, Hill was destitute and more isolated from his family than ever. At a time when other couples might have been contemplating a new, less harried lifestyle as their child-raising years neared an end, Napoleon's marriage was strained to the brink and his relationship with his boys eroded from that of absentee father to distant stranger.

Shame, disgrace, and guilt would all come to Hill eventually, but the overriding emotion of his exile was fear. It was a new and completely disorienting experience for a man who had lived his entire life crashing through walls in a head-lowered charge, nearly oblivious to risk and only fleetingly conscious of the bruises inflicted by immovable objects.

A decade later he could still describe the agony of those months:

> For the first time in my life I knew the pain of constant fear. My previous experiences of defeat had filled my mind with doubt and indecision, but this one filled it with a fear which I seemed unable to remove. . . .
>
> . . . After some months of this my nerves began to crack. My courage had completely left me. The ambition which had heartened me during the long years of labor in search of the causes of failure and success had departed.

Slowly, step by step, I felt myself slipping into a state of lethargy from which I was afraid I would never be able to emerge. . . .

If the seed of insanity had been in my makeup it would have germinated during those . . . months of living death. Foolish indecision, irresolute dreams, doubt and fear were my mind's concern, day and night.

The emergency I faced was disastrous in two ways. First, the very nature of it kept me in a constant state of indecision and fear. Second, the forced concealment kept me in idleness, with its attendant heaviness of time which I naturally devoted to worry. My reasoning faculty had been almost paralyzed. I realized that I had to work myself out of this state of mind. But how? The resourcefulness which had helped me to meet all previous emergencies seemed to have completely taken wing, leaving me helpless.

Out of my difficulties, which were burdensome enough up to this point, grew another which seemed more painful than all the others combined. It was the realization that I had spent the better portion of my life in chasing a rainbow, searching hither and yon for the causes of success, but finding myself now more helpless than any of the thousands I had judged as being failures.

This thought was extremely humiliating. I had lectured all over the country . . . presuming to tell others how to apply the principles of success while here I was, unable to apply them myself. I was sure I could never again face the world with a feeling of confidence.

Every time I looked at myself in a mirror I noticed an expression of self-contempt on my face . . . I had begun to place myself in the category of charlatans who offer others a remedy for failure which they, themselves cannot successfully apply.

In Hill's own mind, his year of exile was the greatest test of his life. Although he never used the parallel himself, the experience was roughly akin to Christ's journey into the wilderness. And the ultimate temptation—to give up, to abandon all he believed in—was all too real for Napoleon. Even after the men who murdered Mellet had been convicted and jailed for life, Hill could not bring himself to come out of hiding.

"The experience had destroyed whatever initiative I possessed," wrote Napoleon. "I felt myself in the clutches of some depressing influences which seemed like a nightmare. I was alive. I could move around. But I could not think of a single move by which I might continue to seek the goal which I had so long ago set for myself. I was rapidly becoming indifferent; worse still, I was becoming grouchy and irritable toward those who had given me shelter in my hour of need."

A bitter, floundering Napoleon Hill remained in West Virginia for several months after danger had passed. His desperate need to begin again seemed hopelessly impossible. His lecture tours and backers and promoters were a distant memory; even if he could afford the time and effort to start up again, the actual financial returns from lecturing were far too modest for a middle-aged man to base a career on. His hopes of publishing his voluminous success course had evaporated with the death of Judge Gary, who had taken ill and died in the months following Mellet's murder.

Then, gradually, Hill's depression bottomed out. A new fear began crowding out his feelings of hopelessness and despair: the fear that this was all there was, that unless he made something happen, he would live out the rest of his years this way. He had not found a safe haven from life's hazards, he had simply quit living altogether. Deep within himself he could not accept life on these terms, and he began struggling to find his way back.

"The turn in my affairs came suddenly in the fall of 1927," wrote Hill. "I left the house one night and walked up to the school building on top of a hill above the village. . . . I began to walk around the building, trying to force my befuddled brain to think clearly. I must have made several hundred trips around the building before anything which even remotely resembled organized thought began to take place in my mind."

When spontaneous thought failed, Hill resorted to a step-by-step review of his own principles of success. Fighting against the part of himself still locked in futility that wanted only to rest, he made himself concentrate, forced his consciousness to go back to the beginning, back nearly twenty years to Andrew Carnegie and the cornerstone of all the other principles he had assembled. A definite major purpose was missing from his life.

As he trudged round and round the school in the starlit night, he tried to conceptualize a definite major purpose grand enough to pursue, worthy enough to achieve, cause enough to once more lower his head and begin charging through walls.

In the crystal-pure air of the November mountain night, Hill's thoughts took him to the brink of mysticism. He dwelled on Carnegie's concept of the "other self"—the capacity of some people faced by crisis to change their habits, to deal with an emergency by finding new dimensions to their persona that fit the situation.

He came to view his ordeal as a testing time, an experience that was forcing him to discover his "other self."

And he mulled over his philosophy, his life's work, his greater purpose in being. He became aware, again, of the fact that he had devoted nearly twenty years to compiling a philosophy, was awed by the improbability of that dedication, was moved by the pent-up positive energy that philosophy could bring to humanity.

He became aware, again, of Carnegie's admonition at the time he accepted the industrialist's challenge: compiling, condensing, and analyzing the principles of success would take at least twenty years. Hill realized he was nearing that epochal deadline.

At length, he was struck by a thought so powerful and enunciated so clearly it was as if a command had been spoken. He would embark for Philadelphia the very next day and get his eight-volume philosophy published.

There were a few technical details that might have stopped other people from following through on the resolution Napoleon reached that night. For openers, he didn't know any publishers or any potential financial backers in Philadelphia. He was also nearly penniless, a condition that made just getting to Philadelphia questionable and staying there for any length of time almost impossible.

But leave he did. Napoleon came down from the hill to have his first really good night's sleep in a year. When he awoke, he began packing and trying to deal with the realities of his decision. He partially resolved the financial problem by borrowing money from his brother-in-law—and eventually from Florence and even his son Blair, who, at age sixteen, was running a profitable backyard poultry and egg business.

It was a half-baked plan, to be sure, seemingly devoid of logic and with no reasonable chance of success. In essence, Napoleon was simply changing addresses, leaving the certainty of food and shelter and an empty life in West Virginia to explore completely unknown prospects in Philadelphia. It was the kind of impulsive gamble that had brought Nap most of his successes and failures, but in the autumn of 1928 it was a risk he needed to take to come alive again.

And come alive he did. Arriving in Philadelphia after driving all night, he set up operations in a comfortable hotel on Locust Street and went to work. He wheedled a local print shop into doing a rush order of fine stationery and business cards with his new address tastefully imprinted in plain bold serif type—the kind of solid, conservative letterhead that suggested NAPOLEON HILL had lived at 1718 Locust Street for years. As soon as he returned home with the stationery, he dashed off a letter to Florence asking her to send him all the sets of his Law of Success texts that were stored in the attic. Ever the organizer, the books he wanted were packed neatly in a shipping crate that had just enough room for Florence to throw in Nap's galoshes—a concession to Philadelphia's November weather and the fact that Napoleon was going to be spending a lot of time in it as he pounded the pavement looking for his big break.

The shipment from Florence arrived about two weeks later; Nap then filled the time with a flurry of activity. He had one set of his Law of Success manuscripts bound in expensive leather covers and the pages embossed in gold. As he waited for the binding to be completed, he spent the better part of two days and nights compiling a list of publishers and business acquaintances to call on, then set to work organizing and rehearsing the presentation he would make.

Then Hill embarked on a dizzying succession of personal calls on Philadelphia publishers and businesses, and telephone calls and letters to out-of-town candidates. His first goal was to find a publisher who would take the book outright, hopefully with a cash advance on royalties. His second, fallback goal was to find a business or entrepreneur who would underwrite the books' publication either through an advance order or as a straight business investment; he calculated that he would need at least twenty-five thousand dollars from such a source to get the books published.

For several weeks Hill poured every ounce of his considerable energy and resourcefulness into face-to-face presentations, telephone calls, and letters. For his efforts he received a landslide of rejections. Book publishers were aghast at the financial risks involved in a fifteen-hundred-page, eight-volume *philosophy* text bearing the name of an author with little or no standing in the commercial book trade. Distribution alone would be a nightmare—the eight-volume sets would be prohibitively expensive, would sell slowly, and would tie up too much merchandizing and warehouse space.

As for private investors, time had seemingly passed by Napoleon. His best prospects were the lions of industry whom he had interviewed over the past twenty years, but many of them were dead and the rest were long since retired. Among his business contacts and the new generation of American entrepreneurs, the promise of Napoleon's elaborate blueprint for success was blunted by the times: in 1928, America's over-revving economy provided such an abundance of wealth and opportunity that success seemed more like a birthright than a goal worth struggling to achieve.

Later in life, Napoleon claimed that he braved the hailstorm of rejections without flinching because of the counseling he received from his "other self." For years thereafter he never spoke or wrote of this aspect of his private struggle lest those he sought to win over think him crazy. But he was not crazy. What he referred to as his "other self" was an alter ego of sorts, a defense mechanism for a man whose only hope for success was to continue believing that he would succeed. It was a part of his personality that engaged exclusively in positive thinking. It functioned much like the mental equivalent of the body's immune system except that the source of its strength was intangible. When the weight of Napoleon's frustrations began beating down his will to continue, his "other self" bombarded his consciousness with positive thoughts born of faith and resolution.

"My reason told me I had exhausted the list [of potential backers]," Hill explained, "but my 'other self' plainly said, 'keep on searching.' "

And he did.

Napoleon Hill's crisis broke shortly after the Thanksgiving of 1928. Late at night, after hours of intense concentration on creating a new list of prospects, he dozed off in his easy chair and let his dreams take him back to his glory years, back to the crackling excitement and personal exuberance of his days on *Hill's Golden Rule*. And suddenly the name of a *Golden Rule* advertiser popped into his mind: Andrew Pelton.

Pelton was a Connecticut-based book publisher who had regularly advertised his self-help books in *Golden Rule*. The connection made in Hill's mind nearly a decade later was a natural. Pelton's leading title in 1919 had been a book called *Power of Will* (by Frank Channing Haddock), which he claimed had "pulled thousands out of the slough of despondency" by teaching them how to "develop an indomitable, irresistible Will." Hill no doubt was familiar with the text and may well have applied some of its lessons in creating what he referred to as his "other self."

As soon as he awoke, Napoleon composed a powerful letter to Pelton, describing the manuscript and his publishing plan. The letter piqued Pelton's interest immediately. He sent Napoleon a telegram to set up an appointment in Philadelphia—to review the manuscript and discuss the plan further.

Sensing victory, Napoleon made sure the meeting produced the results he wanted. The success he had seen for himself a few weeks earlier as he paced around the hilltop school in West Virginia was at hand. He would let nothing stop him now. Quickly, he borrowed another fifty dollars from his brother-in-law and rented a suite in Philadelphia's finest hotel for his meeting with Pelton. He made a grand entrance, striding with starched purposefulness to the registration desk. He flashed a thick roll of cash as he put down the deposit on his room, then strutted to the elevator with the self-assurance of a Rockefeller. Ascending to his suite, he regally dispatched the bellboy to fetch him the tobacconist's most expensive cigars (he rejected the first offering of simply excellent cigars) then tipped the boy four times the going rate for his trouble.

There was method to Napoleon's charade. He wanted Pelton to see him as an immensely successful man, a man whose own accomplishments qualified him as an authority on success—and a man whose manuscript would interest many, many other publishers.

Twenty-four hours later, when Pelton arrived, Hill's name and patrician generosity were known to every clerk and bell-boy on the staff. They treated him and his guest like visiting royalty.

It was a nifty finishing touch to a plan in which every-thing else was already in place. Unlike the other publishers Nap had called on, most of whom specialized in popular or literary works, Pelton knew the potential of the self-help market. He also knew and admired Napoleon and was aware that Nap commanded a sizable following from his magazine and lecturing days. And he knew that Napoleon was an able and indefatigable promoter of his own work. The meeting was brief and to the point.

"When he came I showed him the original manuscripts of my philosophy and briefly explained what I believed its mission to be," said Hill. "He turned through the pages of the manuscripts for a few minutes, stopped suddenly and fixed his eyes on the wall for a few seconds, then said, 'I will publish your books for you.' "

The two men quickly worked out an agreement. Pelton would provide the capital and see to the printing and distri-bution of the book. Napoleon would perform necessary rewrites and contribute his considerable promotional ener-gies to the success of the project. And Napoleon got a much needed advance on royalties on the spot.

★ ★ ★

"I am still feeling in the 1910 mood," Hill wrote Florence in a letter some months later. His "1910 mood" began as soon as the meeting with Pelton ended. The buoyancy and grit that had carried Napoleon from West Virginia to that meeting quickly flamed into uninhibited optimism and confidence— and unleashed the inspired passion he had brought to his courtship of Florence and to the birth of *Hill's Golden Rule* so many years before.

Napoleon celebrated his rebirth by working even harder than he had before. He dashed off samples of the original text to many of the great minds he had consulted during its creation . . . men like Thomas Edison, newspaper tycoon Cyrus Curtis, retailing giant F. W. Woolworth, former president Woodrow Wilson, and former president William H. Taft, then chief justice of the Supreme Court.

Two of these men—Taft and Curtis—responded within a week or two. Each promised to eventually read the entire manuscript, and each praised a specific section of the book. By the time the book went to press, all of them had come forth with endorsements that gave Hill and Pelton the legitimacy they needed for their trade and retail promotions.

Each giant's remarks were reprinted with permission in the first edition of *Law of Success* and have appeared in every edition since. Like the text itself, the names of the endorsers would remain significant to success-minded people for decades to come.

After posting the sample copies, Napoleon locked himself away for twelve or eighteen hours a day, rewriting, updating, and condensing his huge manuscript. It was a daunting task, even for a prolific writer and expert typist. Banging away at the battered old upright typewriter he'd kept with him since his *Hill's Golden Rule* days, he ground out page after page of the rewrite. He was copy editor, proofreader, writer, and typist all rolled into one. The pages that rolled off his typewriter were grammatically immaculate, the typing nearly flawless, the style vintage Hill: lively, passionate, soul-stirring.

Napoleon's rewrite began in the last weeks of 1927. His work, including final editing, was completed March 26, 1928. He celebrated by typing a two-page letter to Florence in which he described the just-completed work as "100% better than before." In the same letter, Napoleon announced that he had taken a position as the general sales manager for a car dealership in West Philadelphia in order to generate income until the royalties started pouring in. His eager expectations for royalties were a sure sign that he was "still feeling in a 1910 mood."

"The royalties on the course will not begin to come in for two or three months, and the big returns will not come in before next Fall," he wrote, "but the thing is under way and the plans we have worked out almost insure me an income . . . of at least $1,000 a month after it gets underway. I will buy a country home for you out of the first accumulation, and then we will begin to store a goodly sum of the remainder in the bank so I will never again be in the position of having to accept 'alms' as I did last year. I am cured of that forever."

As always, Napoleon misjudged how long it would take for his work to produce revenue, as well as how much revenue it would produce. The first trickle of royalties began in the summer of 1928, as promised, but the big royalty checks didn't come in until early in 1929. And when the big checks came, they came very big. Nap may never have received a $1,000 royalty check for *Law of Success*. Early in 1929, his royalties averaged $2,500 a month, a princely income for the times.

Despite the unexpected wealth that finally came to them, the interim period created ever more stress for the Hill marriage. Florence had been forced to support the family entirely by herself for the year Napoleon spent in hiding with her relatives. She and Blair and her relatives had funded his come-back. Nap's advance lasted just long enough to finish work on the manuscript. His job with the car dealership initially promised the kind of financial support the family desperate-ly needed, but then Nap quit in the summer of 1928, in anticipation of royalty income.

The couple's correspondence in 1928 suggested a mar-riage slipping into crisis. Most of Nap's letters were to the boys; those he wrote to Florence were filled with images of what they would do with the wealth that awaited them, and pleas for her to write him something more than a perfunc-tory note.

Adding to Florence's problems were her housing arrange-ments. Perhaps because she owed her family so much for their support of her and the boys, Florence had agreed to live with her mother, an aged woman who, according to other members of the family, was ill-tempered and domineering. In several of his letters, Napoleon's attempt to rally Florence's spirits focused on opportunities for her to get away from her mother for a while.

If, indeed, Florence found living with her mother diffi-cult, she must have been desperate for good news by the time Napoleon quit his car dealership job in the summer of 1928. At the end of March she had lost her last means of escape from the house—the car she used for shopping and errands. It was demolished when Florence skidded off a country bridge one day; miraculously, she suffered relatively minor injuries . . . except to her morale.

The endless wait for the big royalty checks to start coming in may have discouraged Florence and surprised Napoleon, but that was only because of Nap's naive forecasts and Florence's flagging faith in his ability to succeed. In fact, *Law of Success* was a near-instant hit; the pattern of royalty checks simply reflected the time it took to establish distribution, supply modest inventories to retailers to test demand, then ship reorders, the quantity of which were based on initial sales.

For *Law of Success,* the initial sales were brisk—incredibly so considering the cost of the books. Each title in the eight-volume set sold for about four dollars; the cost of the complete set was more than thirty dollars—enough to feed a family of four for a month in 1929. Nevertheless, the books sold well, and booksellers reordered aggressively.

As it happened, the very characteristics of the manuscript that had scared off conventional book publishers made *Law of Success* a classic. It was unique for readers and retailers alike. Its encyclopedic scope set it apart from the steady stream of self-help titles that passed in and out of public vogue. Its philosophical dimension offered the scholarly and the successful something to ponder. Its instructional format— Napoleon always thought of *Law of Success* as a course, not a book—offered the struggling masses practical, step-by-step advice for getting ahead. And it was all tied to the compelling pragmatism of Carnegie's original concept: The entire work revolved around the collective wisdom of America's most successful—colossally successful—leaders of commerce and industry. The "laws" set forth in *Law of Success* were not theory, they were fact and testimony, the gospel of capitalism for the individual. Nothing like it had ever been published before.

Even the ponderous, pricey multivolume format of the original *Law of Success* offered unique benefits to readers and retailers. For readers, it meant the huge set could be purchased one volume at a time, in affordable chunks. For retailers, *Law of Success* was a forerunner of the modern-day continuity series: customers who bought Volume I usually came back for Volume II, then Volume III, and so on. Sales of Volumes II through VIII could be accurately projected according to sales of the previous volumes, which made the set less risky to handle than many other titles. Furthermore,

Napoleon Hill's father,
James Monroe Hill,
as a young man in the
1890s. At the urging of his
second wife, who also had
a tremendous influence on
Napoleon, the elder Hill
taught himself dentistry
and established a
successful practice.

Napoleon Hill was
just twenty-one years old—
and still known as Oliver Napoleon—
when this photo was taken in 1904
in Wise County, Virginia.

Napoleon Hill's education began in Wise County's
one room Laurel Grove School.

Florence Horner
strikes a gentle pose for a
portrait believed taken
in 1908, shortly
before her marriage
to Napoleon Hill.

Flora Elizabeth (Hood) Horner,
Florence's mother, was still the
strong-willed matriarch of
the Horner clan when this photo
was taken in Orlando, Florida,
about 1925.

Napoleon and sons
Jimmy (right) and Blair,
circa 1915. Blair's long hair
disguised the fact that he was
born without ears.

Napoleon Hill on a
Washington, D. C., patio in 1934,
during the time he served as an
adviser to FDR. Though he
appears to be much younger,
he was fifty-one years old.

David H. Hill,
Napoleon's third son,
was a twenty-three-year-old
platoon sergeant stationed in
Alaska when this picture was
taken in 1941, just six weeks
before Pearl Harbor.

Blair Hill,
Napoleon's second son,
was a successful merchant
and civic leader when
this photo was taken in
the early 1960s.

Hill's mentor, Andrew Carnegie, made a small fortune in railroads, then a colossal one as a pioneer in America's steel industry.

Charged by Carnegie with distilling the essence of success through interviews with American leaders, Hill met with many, including Henry Ford, presidents Taft and Wilson, and the great inventor Thomas Alva Edison (shown here).

From the Laboratory of Thomas A. Edison. Orange. NJ

My dear Mr. Hill:

Allow me to express my appreciation of the compliment you have paid me in sending me the original manuscript of the LAW OF SUCCESS philosophy.

From a cursory examination of your manuscript I can see that you have spent a great deal of time and thought in its preparation. Your philosophy is sound and you are to be congratulated for sticking to your work in organizing it, over so long a period of years. If your students of this philosophy will work as hard in applying it as you have in building it they will be amply rewarded for their labor

It will not be possible for me to read your manuscripts as carefully as they deserve to be read, as I'am going to Florida, shortly, where I shall spend several months in continuance of my investigations in connection with rubber

Yours very truly,

Thos A. Edison

Edison wrote this letter to Hill shortly before *Law of Success* was published. Hill and his publisher had sent advance copies of the work to luminaries like Edison to secure endorsements for promoting the title.

By 1920, Hill was the self-assured, thirty-seven-year-old editor of *Napoleon Hill's Magazine.*

Hill's first commercial success in spreading his philosophy of achievement came with the magazine *Hill's Golden Rule.* His joy was short-lived, however. Contentious business partners forced him out.

With *Napoleon Hill's Magazine,* Hill showed that he had learned his lessons from earlier defeat, and the periodical flourished. The largest cover line promised a circulation of 300,000 by the end of 1922, a goal Hill probably never met.

Rosa Lee Hill, Napoleon's second wife, flashes her winning smile for a Florida newspaper in 1939. The couple had just purchased a castle-like estate in Mount Dora, Florida, with earnings from *Think and Grow Rich!*

California-bound Napoleon and Annie Lou Hill visit friends in Toccoa, Georgia, shortly after their wedding in 1943.

This mid–fifties photograph shows Hill with the old L. C. Smith typewriter on which he wrote *Law of Success* in the twenties, and all his subsequent works.

Inspired by W. Clement Stone, Hill abandoned his retirement to once again promote his philosophy. *Success Unlimited* magazine debuted in 1954 as part of Napoleon Hill Associates' efforts to reinforce the teachings of the Science of Success. It later became an independent publishing venture.

Hill addresses a packed house for a 1959 Science of Success course in Chicago.

K. Duane Hurley (left), president of Salem College in West Virginia, stands beside Napoleon Hill in 1957 after conferring on him an honorary doctorate of literature.

W. Clement Stone (left) and Napoleon Hill promote their newly published book, *Success Through a Positive Mental Attitude*, at a Chicago bookstore in 1960.

the book helped increase retail traffic; those who bought Volume I were likely to return to the store seven more times to complete their set.

Volume I of the *Law of Success* was a flawed, rambling, sometimes incomprehensible document that a skilled text editor with a strong sense of book market imperatives might have condensed to a slick, fast-reading, fifty-page chapter. Indeed, the other seven volumes were similarly flawed, though to a more modest degree. But reduced to safe, conventional publishing practices, *Law of Success* would most likely have been a very ordinary book with a very temporary life. Its imperfect, unvarnished defiance of convention was part of its raw power and freshness. These qualities would remain through four different editions, countless printings, and more than sixty years of active sales.

The first volume of *Law of Success* laid out the Carnegie concept, a brief history of Hill's struggles to compile and publish the work, and a synopsis of his fifteen principles of success. The power and promise of Hill's principles, or "laws," came through clearly:

A Definite Chief Aim spoke of the focus and dedication that success requires, and Hill promised to teach the reader how to conceive a worthwhile main goal.

Self Confidence was different from egotism; it required mastery of the six basic fears—poverty, poor health, old age, criticism, loss of love, and death; Hill's chapter on self-confidence would give the reader a mixture of facts, anecdotes, and pure inspiration to use in confronting these fears.

Habit of Saving addressed the need to accumulate capital in a free-enterprise society; Hill's chapter on the subject would teach readers "how to distribute income systematically."

Initiative and Leadership were widely recognized requirements for success; Hill's instruction would cover how to develop leadership qualities and instincts in oneself.

Imagination covered the power of creativity in any career; Hill's chapter would show how to develop and apply one's own imagination.

And so it went through the other ten laws of success: Enthusiasm, Self Control, Habit of Doing More than Paid for, Pleasing Personality, Accurate Thinking, Concentration, Profiting by Failure, Tolerance, and Napoleon's favorite, Practicing the Golden Rule.

The main lesson of Volume I dealt with Napoleon's Master Mind principle, a pragmatic expansion of the old axiom, Two heads are better than one. Hill's definition of the Master Mind was "a mind that is developed through the harmonious cooperation of two or more people who ally themselves for the purpose of accomplishing a single task." If the concept wasn't unique, Hill's application of it to business was: The Master Mind Alliance required not only commitment to goals but also to the roles each individual in the alliance would play and the strategies and tactics they would pursue. The Master Mind Alliance eliminated the main causes of conflict between business associates, clearing the way for them to direct all their energies to the challenges of the marketplace.

Decades later, business consultants would espouse the same principle using the analogy of a laser beam that creates power by focusing seemingly modest amounts of energy on a single target. The beauty of Hill's Master Mind principle was that it could be applied to marriages, families, and careers as well as business and social organizations. Indeed, W. Clement Stone, then the twenty-six-year-old owner of a growing insurance business in Chicago, would one day teach his salespeople to form a Master Mind Alliance with their spouses so that the demands of success in a sales career would unite their marriages rather than cause the disintegration of either the marriage or the career.

But Volume I of *Law of Success* went well beyond pedestrian explanations of the Master Mind principle. It served notice to readers that this "course" and its teacher would not be bound by conventional dogma. To relate the laws of success to the laws of nature, Napoleon drew parallels to molecules, atoms, and electrons, then pursued an elaborate metaphysical discourse on "the vibrating fluid of matter" that spoke of the existence of a universal medium—ether—in which the thought waves of humankind vibrate more or less eternally, available to be received by open-minded people and applied to current living.

Law of Success might well have been discarded as the ravings of a lunatic but for the fact that much of Hill's most improbable conjecture was spun from the musings of men like Thomas Edison and Alexander Graham Bell. Thus anchored in respectability, these passages stimulated readers to wonder, to ponder life on a grander scale more than any self-help book ever has, before or since.

And *Law of Success* boldly encroached on two institutions of the day. Hill bluntly ridiculed educators who defined education as the imparting of knowledge. Education, said Hill, does not stop with the passive accumulation of knowledge. To have value, education must also include learning to organize knowledge, classify it, and put it into action. "An 'educated' person," wrote Hill, "is one who knows how to acquire everything he needs in the attainment of his main purpose in life, without violating the rights of his fellow men."

The anecdote he offered to underscore this lesson concerned testimony given by Henry Ford in a libel suit he brought against a newspaper for profiling him as an "ignoramus." According to Hill, the newspaper's attorney grilled Ford on his command of history, geography, and other school disciplines for an hour until Ford finally tired of it.

"If I should really wish to answer the foolish questions you have just asked, or any of the others you have been asking," Ford said, "let me remind you that I have a row of electronic push buttons hanging over my desk and by placing my finger on the right button I could call in men who could give me the correct answer to all the questions you have asked and to many that you have not the intelligence either to ask or answer."

The moral, said Nap: You don't have to know all the answers, you have to know how to get answers to the questions that count.

Educators probably took less exception to Hill's criticism of their field than did some religious leaders when he spoke of the Bible. Napoleon distinguished between "Nature's Bible" and the Bible used in organized religion. He criticized the latter by defining the former.

"[Nature's Bible] is above and beyond the power of man to alter. Moreover, it tells its story not in the ancient dead languages or hieroglyphics of half-savage races, but in universal language which all who have eyes may read. Nature's Bible, from which we have derived all the knowledge that is worth knowing, is one that no man may alter or in any manner tamper with."

There is no record that Hill's sentiments about the Bible and organized religion produced any public controversy, but *Law of Success* and some of Hill's later works drew heated letters from the faithful in ample abundance.

Long-dreamed-of wealth began flowing into the Hill family coffers early in 1929. At the end of January, a jubilant Napoleon composed a four-page typewritten letter from New York City to Florence chronicling how he intended to handle a spate of business opportunities that had come his way on the strength of his books' early success.

A Long Island real-estate business owned by a friend of Florence was courting Nap to train and manage its sales force. The offer included salary, commission, and commission overrides that would be worth $250 a week—a very com-

fortable income by itself in 1929 and, combined with his royalty checks, a ticket to plentiful living.

Nap turned down the real estate job to take advantage of
opportunities he had with Bernard MacFadden, owner of the
New York Evening Graphic and a stable of mass-circulating
magazines. Hill's dealings with MacFadden went back to the
early twenties when the two shared the speaker's podium at
an Iowa business school. Hill subsequently had written on
success for MacFadden's publications at various times over
the years. Then, with the successful debut of *Law of Success,*
MacFadden contracted Napoleon to write a daily success
column for the *Evening Graphic.* The column was itself an
instant success and MacFadden was taking it into syndication.
Replies from other newspapers were so brisk they expected
daily syndication receipts of one hundred dollars within a
month. The catch was, MacFadden's editors wanted Nap
to devote full time to the column and a new MacFadden
magazine.

As part of the deal, MacFadden offered to sell the *Law of
Success* via direct-response ads in his mass-circulation magazines. Such promotion promised high-volume sales of the
books—and larger-still royalty checks for Nap.

"All in all," concluded Napoleon, "I think the Wheel of
Fate is turning up some very nice paddles opposite me, and
the chances are that this still stands a mighty good show of
being the banner year of my life by miles and miles."

Indeed, it was all that and more. Within weeks of the
posting of that letter, the big royalty checks began rolling in
and Napoleon and Florence were glorying in undreamed of
wealth. After years of humiliation and want, Florence suddenly had hundreds of dollars a week to support her household. And Nap, having spent most of his adult life trying to
project an image of wealth and success even when destitute,
had access to hundreds more dollars to invest in long-held
business fantasies and to support the cosmopolitan lifestyle he

cherished. Now he could afford the tobacconist's most expensive cigars every day, and stay in the best hotel in town as a matter of course. He had always worn stylish, finely tailored suits, but now he could afford as many of them as he wanted. And for a man who had always loved automobiles—the bigger and more expensive, the better—1929 brought a previously unthinkable milestone: Nap bought his first Rolls-Royce.

For nearly a year, the Hill family soared through life on clouds of ecstasy. Letters between Florence and Napoleon were warm and happy. They met often for romantic weekends. They laughed and dreamed together, took the boys on picnics and lighthearted outings. And in the summer of 1929, Nap made good on a dream they had all shared for more than a decade—he bought a nice place in the country where the Hill family finally came to live together under one roof.

Napoleon's "nice place in the country" was, of course, no mere house or farm—nor was it just a home. It was a pristine, wooded fiefdom that sprawled over six hundred acres of idyllic meadowlands in New York's Catskill Mountains. The rambling mansion stood three stories high, each level completely encircled by whitewashed veranda. The mansion's circular drive occupied the better part of an acre in its own right, and the building was flanked by a series of solid brick outbuildings—each destined in Napoleon's mind to play a role in his next great commercial undertaking. Together, these buildings formed an aristocratic colony perched on the shores of a small lake. Farther away were the stables, footpaths into the hardwood stands, trickling mountain brooks, and sites for tennis courts. The view was filled with the dense green heights of the Catskill Mountains.

While this opulent estate would be the home Nap had always promised—ease and prestige for Florence, ponies and streams for the boys—it would also be the stage for one of Napoleon's grandest concepts. Hill procured the estate along with several large investors with the intention of turning it into the world's first University-sized Success School, complete with bucolic campus, lecture halls, and a carefully chosen faculty. Eventually, they intended to also build and sell vacation homes on the grounds for successful people who wanted to mix traditional vacation pleasures with the opportunity to brush up on the principles that would enhance their continued success.

In contrast to some of Napoleon's previous epic-sized visions, this one captured the imaginations of many people— particularly the publisher of the *Catskill Mountain Star,* a newspaper serving Saugerties, Woodstock, Phoenicia, and dozens of small villages and tiny hamlets in the Catskills. The June 28, 1929, edition of the *Star* characterized the purchase of the estate by Hill and his associates as "the greatest [deal] put over in the Catskill Mountains in many years." The newspaper also disclosed that its own publisher had been instrumental in wooing Hill to locate his school in the region.

The *Star's* treatment of Hill was dramatic testimony to how persuasive Napoleon's self-promotion had become, now that it was supported by his celebrity status as a rich and famous author:

> Mr. Hill is well known to the people of America, and to thousands of his followers and students now living in every civilized country on earth. He is Success Editor of the *New York Evening Graphic,* and his success column . . . reaches several million readers every day. He is the author of a world famous philosophy [known as] *The Law of Success.* . . .
>
> . . . He was born in the midst of poverty and illiteracy, but despite this handicap he has managed to put himself beyond the need of money, is one of the best educated men living, has spread his work and his fame entirely around this earth, and . . . his best work is yet to be done. . . .

. . . Perhaps no other man in America could have brought to this community as many advantages as will Mr. Hill. Mr. Hill's advertising program is international in scope . . . [and he] spends large amounts of money for advertising.

The *Star* also detailed the scope of Napoleon's plans for the world's first "Success Colony":

Mr. Hill will build two additional lakes on the place, remodel the clubhouse, and generally beautify the place.

The . . . property will be used as a summer colony for Mr. Hill's students who will come there yearly from all parts of the world, for personal training in the famous *Law of Success* philosophy. Summer lecture courses will be conducted by Mr. Hill and his staff of teachers. The large building near the clubhouse will be converted into a first class lecture hall and instruction building. Additional buildings for this purpose will be erected as needed.

A school for boys will be started on the place next year that will be in session all the year. In the summer the boys will be taught how to make the soil productive. They will be thoroughly trained . . . in physical culture, proper eating, right methods of exercising, etc. Every boy must work both his body and his mind, no matter how much money his parents spend on him.

Having proved, over a period of more than 12 years of practical demonstration, that he can make successful men out of failures, Mr. Hill now proposes to demonstrate that he can insure boys against failure in the first place, by giving them the right sort of schooling. . . .

. . . Mr. Hill will publish a national magazine that will be circulated in every state, city, town and village in

America. This publication will . . . place this town on the map all over the country.

In July 1929, Napoleon, Florence, and the boys moved into their genteel new home. It was the most glorious summer the family had ever experienced. Work was already underway to convert the buildings to their intended purposes. Napoleon busied himself supervising and cranking out the first edition of *Top O' The World,* a sixteen-page, tabloid-size promotional publication heralding the formation and mission of his revolutionary Success Colony, and describing Napoleon's own life struggles and the creation of the Principles of Success that led to the colony's formation.

For the first time in their lives, the Hill boys actually lived with their father and spent long hours in his company. Napoleon took them hiking far into the woods, teaching them animal calls, tracking, and other facets of woodsmanship he had learned as a boy in Wise County. At night he demonstrated his prowess with the fiddle and piano.

The boys learned about his stern side, too. Years later, David recounted one of Napoleon's favorite forms of punishment—making the guilty boy clear rocks from the fields. It was rough, dull work with no apparent purpose, at least to the boys. Nap's ultimate goal undoubtedly was to clear land for tilling, but the fields were littered with so many rocks that, as far as the boys were concerned, there was no hope of clearing them in a lifetime. The boys might have shared Napoleon's undaunted enthusiasm for accomplishing the inconceivable but for the fact that Nap himself never touched a rock nor took to the soil with a spade or hoe. Nearing his forty-fifth birthday, Napoleon had at long last achieved the fame and fortune that he had dreamed of during the backbreaking labors of his youth; there was no way he would again take to manual labor, no matter how enthusiastically he would recommend it to others. David would later say that he never saw his father do any kind of physical labor.

But Napoleon's disciplinary measures were more than counterbalanced by the pony rides, swimming and fishing, evening songfests, and Nap's spellbinding storytelling. The Hill family became closer and happier than ever before.

Summer inevitably gave way to fall, however. With the changing of colors in the hills came another change in the family. It began with Napoleon leaving more and more often to deliver speeches and lectures. These appearances were, on the one hand, the price of success. Nap was in demand, and his soul-moving oratory sold books, kept his name before the public, and fulfilled his obligations to his publisher. But his speaking engagements offered something else, too, something Nap needed: a refuge from the pastoral quiet of the Catskills. He craved the excitement of the city, the electric tension of an expectant audience, the backslapping hustle of business meetings, and the social pomp of being seen at the right restaurants with the right people at the right time.

By the time the leaves began to change color in the Catskills, Napoleon was back on the speaking tour loop. His departure may have caused some disappointment to Florence and the boys, but there were greater disappointments to come.

Like Napoleon Hill's own life, the manic American economy had ascended to unthinkable heights of prosperity in 1929, much of it pouring from the stock market. Newspapers offered a plentiful fare of rags-to-riches stories involving common people parlaying modest, hard-earned savings into fortunes large and small. One typical story of the day told how a broker's valet made margin purchases of stocks recommended by his boss—and quickly converted a savings account created from nickel-and-dime tips into a $250,000 fortune. A similar story told how a nurse put her savings into stocks recommended by a patient and made $30,000 in less than a year.

Even if those stories were laced with newsstand-selling hyperbole, incredible fortunes were being made in the U.S. securities market in 1928 and 1929. Hot stocks like RCA actually quadrupled in value in the course of a year. Samuel Insull, owner of a vast empire of utility companies and one of Hill's *Law of Success* acquaintances, had a fifty-day run in which the value of his securities increased by an estimated rate of seven thousand dollars *per minute*, twenty-four hours a day.

But as Napoleon took to the road, the stock market was twitching and flopping nervously. For more than a year government and financial leaders had issued public warnings that stocks were overvalued and those trading them were dangerously over-leveraged. September of 1929 brought several panic-selling plunges in the market—always followed by rallies as speculators swooped in to buy low, confident they could sell high in a few days and accumulate ever larger fortunes. For the confident and aggressive, the plunges were an opportunity. So was margin buying—buying stocks with a combination of a little cash and a lot of credit.

On October 3—about the time Nap was reestablishing his New York City office—panic selling hit a highwater mark. In the last hour of New York Stock Exchange trading, 1.5 million shares were sold and prices plunged. Even steel stocks felt the heat, declining ten points that day. Two days later, the market had recovered, then plunged again on October 15, recovered the next day, then crashed in just two hours of trading on October 18. A jittery recovery began the next day and continued into October 23.

As Nap sat down to lunch that day—three days prior to his forty-fifth birthday—he was well aware of the nerve-wracking melodrama being played out on Wall Street.

On October 23, the market's nervous recovery ended at lunch; in the afternoon, panic set in again and six million shares—a week's worth of trading volume in normal times—were sold at bargain-basement prices. Not a stock trader himself, Napoleon watched the economic story of the century unfold without realizing how it would affect his own life.

The next day, nearly thirteen million shares were traded on the New York Stock Exchange, for a net loss of three million dollars in share values. On Monday, October 28, nine million shares were traded, and NYSE stock values fell by a gut-wrenching fourteen million dollars. Police cordoned off Wall Street and full-scale panic set in.

On Tuesday, October 29, 1929, the U.S. economy was wiped out. Hysterical shareholders sold for any price they could get. Trading volume on the New York Stock Exchange passed sixteen million shares, and prices sank out of sight. In one day, the value of NYSE stocks fell an incredible *ten billion dollars*—more than twice the amount of currency then in circulation in the United States.

It was the most cataclysmic single day in U.S. economic history. Years later, historians would estimate that between one million and three million Americans felt the effects of the stock market crash immediately—not just traders and speculators who lost paper fortunes, but legions of unsuspecting citizens whose savings accounts were obliterated in bank failures or whose leveraged purchases were lost in loan calls by desperate financial institutions. And thousands lost their jobs immediately.

For tens of millions more, Napoleon and his family among them, the full impact of the crash was delayed for weeks or months. Indeed, years later Napoleon recalled his feelings of disassociation with the despair that enveloped New York during the days surrounding the crash. "I was amused," he wrote, "at the actions of people who had been so diligently trying to get something for nothing by gambling on stock margins but who had actually gotten nothing for something with surprising speed. . . . I was little impressed by what was happening. I was sure it would blow over and the world would right itself inside of a few months."

Napoleon finished out 1929 lecturing in New York City and working on another book, *The Magic Ladder to Success.* Sales of *Law of Success* abruptly slowed to a trickle, of course, but Hill, like most Americans, still expected the fallout from the crash to be a short-lived slump. President Herbert Hoover convinced industrialists not to cut wages and further propped up the economy by instituting a small tax cut and a modest increase in public works spending. On New Year's Eve, the Department of Labor predicted that 1930 would be a "splendid employment year."

It was not, of course. Great chunks of the nation's investment capital were disappearing from the economy as foreign investors transferred funds into European banks to take advantage of high interest rates subsidized by governments that were, themselves, trying to fend off economic collapse. As demand for consumer products worsened in the United States, industrialists maintained wages but cut jobs, and consumer spending continued to spiral down at a sickening rate. And as the nation's industrial economy ground to a halt, a debilitating drought spread across America's croplands.

Historians estimate the total financial losses stemming from the crash of 1929 and the subsequent depression at fifty billion dollars. By 1932 the land of opportunity was a graveyard of shattered dreams. By 1933 one out of four wage earners was out of work, and many of the rest had settled for menial, low-paying jobs. Tenant farmers and sharecroppers lost their land and streamed into cities, only to take their place with other desperate victims of the times in soup lines and "Hoovervilles"—clusters of ramshackle huts and shanties constructed and inhabited by destitute squatters.

As of May 8, 1930, the Hill family was relatively untouched by the economic convulsions sweeping America. Florence and the boys were back in Lumberport, but only out of preference for the local schools and living close to friends and family. Napoleon wrote to Florence that day from his office in New York City to celebrate the romantic interlude they had just shared and his glowing prospects for continued success. Wrote Nap, "You were so slim and nice, and above all, you were so jolly and effervescent . . . that everybody fell in love with you all over again, including yours truly."

On the business front, he had organized his lecture series into a class and his new book, *The Magic Ladder to Success,* was at press. "I am looking forward to [the new book] with anticipation as it will bring me hundreds of new students and new contacts which I so badly need," Napoleon wrote Florence. "This old crowd has been worked out."

He saw no great cause for concern, however. He spoke of how thankful he was to be "on top once more" and described his latest side enterprise with an otherwise unidentifiable colleague whose fast disappearance from Hill's life indicated how rapidly optimistic plans succumbed to the new national mood:

Mr. North is writing a new moving picture play, based upon Lincoln's life, making use of the *Law of Success* principles, and he believes it will be a winner. Everyone who has heard of it thinks the same. It is my play and will be produced by the Parks. They think it will be good for $2,000,000 at least. What a lot of money! I see it in the cards that this is to be my very best year financially, although it did not start off so well. However, the work

I did out West is proving to have laid a foundation for me . . . that will be very valuable a little later. . . ."

Within a few months, however, the wolves were at the Hill family door. *The Magic Ladder to Success* had been released to a public that was increasingly preoccupied with survival. A growing number of Americans could no long afford the luxury of a book, particularly not one dedicated to exploiting opportunities that no longer existed. Commercially the book was virtually stillborn. Worse still, sales of *Law of Success* were trickling to a near halt, too. Nap's royalty checks declined from magnificent four-figure denominations to mere grocery money—and less. The checks to Florence from Andrew Pelton amounted to only $53 in August, $21 in September, and just $15 in October. Hill was still writing his success column, but the once-promising syndication drive was stuck at just forty newspapers, many of which were slipping into their own financial desperation.

By early October 1930, the Hill family's brief fling with prosperity and wealth was over, and they were in more severe financial straits than ever. Florence once again went on the family dole to keep the boys clothed and fed, and Napoleon had to pawn her engagement ring to meet his own expenses. He had long since defaulted on the Catskill property. The owner held off foreclosure as Nap searched frantically through his network of once-wealthy friends and contacts for a financial savior. But it was not to be. The few financiers who had survived the onset of the depression were far too pragmatic to invest in a private school with a dubious curriculum and an impossibly remote location. The Hill family's Eden—and Napoleon's dreams of a university of success—slid over the precipice before the year ended.

In a letter to Florence dated October 5, 1930, Napoleon

tried to sound optimistic about his latest strategies for success. One concerned a movie his friend and associate Lester Parks was working on, the other was a promotion for *Law of Success* inspired by equal parts of desperation and naïveté. Hill described the latter this way:

> I am working on a plan now to offer a free college education . . . to the high school student who sends in the best idea for a plot for a moving picture based upon any of the ideas in the *Law of Success* textbooks. We plan to organize a sales force and take the contest to all the high schools all over the country. If I get it over it will make me rich in a year. If I do not I might go to jail. . . . The idea is that every contestant would need the *Law of Success* textbooks in order to get ideas from them for the contest.

Napoleon had employed the same sales incentive concept during his *Napoleon Hill's Magazine* days with no success, and he would have none in 1930 either. Nor would anything come of his motion picture interests. Like America itself, Napoleon suddenly found himself without even a dream, let alone the means to pursue it.

Like tears shed into a lifeless ocean, the days of Napoleon Hill's life slid unnoticed, one after the other, into the dark oblivion of 1931 and 1932. It wasn't for lack of noble effort or stronghearted determination on his part, however.

Early in 1931, Hill set out to reawaken his countrymen's spirits and his own sagging fortunes. In March, the first issue of the digest-sized *Inspiration Magazine* hit the street. The magazine was published by the auspicious-sounding International Success Society. Its forty pages were written, edited, laid out, and produced by Napoleon Hill, who was also the president, founder, and sole employee of the society. *Inspiration* was a maverick publication from cover to cover. It contained no ads and no feature stories; the first thirty pages were filled with brief tidbits of advice, inspiration, anecdotes, and quotes—more than a hundred of them. Nearly all the rest of the pages were filled with "The Question Box," an advice column in which Hill answered questions supposedly sent in by readers. Napoleon himself created the questions, then answered them in a style that ranged from blunt to caustic:

> Q. My ambition is to make a fortune and make it quickly, and I am not so particular how I do it. What can you do for me?
>
> A. See Al Capone and change your address to the County jail. . . .
>
> Q. My boy will not work, except when trying to get money out of me; then he works altogether too hard. How can I interest him in earning his own money?
>
> A. Try putting him on a fast until he goes to work. Hunger will often do more than words to persuade a boy to work.

As an advice columnist, Napoleon probably mirrored the national mood as well or better than any writer of the times. However, few Americans were willing to spend twenty-five cents to be inspired by Hill or any other layman, and *Inspiration* disappeared after two issues.

Characteristically, Hill was not discouraged. In April 1931, sensing a resurgence in the economy, he launched a comeback of his own. He moved his base of operations to Washington, D.C., and created the International Publishing Corporation of America, another auspicious-sounding organization whose assets consisted of the right to purchase at cost copies of Hill's books that lay unsold in several warehouses. But selling books was only a modest part of his plan.

Along with some associates, he sunk thousands of dollars into promoting his "Mental Dynamite" lectures in the area. The plan: Sell the lectures, sell the books, and, most of all, sell stocks in the International Publishing Corporation of America.

"This is the biggest advertising campaign ever placed back of a lecturer," he told Florence. "I don't see how we can misfire. This is a fine city for my work, with all of these thousands of government clerks who are looking for some way out. We count on a class of no less than one hundred. It might easily surprise us and run as high as five hundred. We are charging $20 for the course. One hundred will see us clear with a profit of $500 or $600, and in addition, a fine list of people to whom we can sell our stock, which is the main thing we are interested in accomplishing at this time."

Soon thereafter he created a related organization, International Success University. Under this banner he launched *Success Magazine* in October.

But Napoleon was premature in his optimism about the economy, which would not bottom out until 1933 and which would even then recover in agonizing inches. In the early thirties, the depression yielded success to few, and Napoleon was not to be among them. His lectures yielded just enough money for him to scrape by—most of the time. Occasionally, he had to "borrow" from Florence just to pay for food and shelter. Entire months went by with no royalty checks at all from sales of his books. When they came at all, the checks usually were for less than twenty dollars.

Like Franklin Delano Roosevelt, who was then campaigning for the presidency, Hill believed the nation's economic woes in 1931 and 1932 stemmed from the public's lack of confidence in America and its institutions. He would later take credit for coining the phrase, "We have nothing to fear but fear itself."

Whether he actually created that line or not, Hill believed

it and put together several schemes in 1931 and 1932 to shake Americans out of their mental lethargy. He directed a fifty-thousand-dollar membership campaign for the Keystone Automobile Club in Philadelphia, which failed, then a three-month radio campaign to stop the run on banks, which failed, then a promotional campaign in Baltimore to restore faith in financial institutions in that city . . . which also failed.

Hill blamed each failure on the lack of confidence of his sponsors, but in fact public despair was so deeply and widely ingrained in the American psyche that one man, company, or city could not poke a hole in the spreading gloom. It would take the entire federal government to achieve that, and it would take years, not weeks or months, to get America going again.

In 1933, the year Napoleon would turn fifty years old, he came to grips with the reality of his—and America's—situation. There was no fortune waiting for him to claim during those difficult times, and, by himself, he could not change the times. He settled in to support himself as best he could through lectures and the sale of an occasional article, and waited for the depression to pass.

But Hill's passivity was not to last very long. Shortly before his fiftieth birthday, he was contacted by the Roosevelt administration. Acting on the strong personal recommendation of Congressman Jennings Randolph, one of Hill's longtime admirers who wielded great influence in the New Deal reform program, the administration wanted Hill to join the White House staff as an adviser, speechwriter, and public relations man for the National Recovery Administration.

It was a strange fit of man and organization. The NRA was Roosevelt's primary weapon against the depression. Its primary legislative mandate was to restore "balance" to the national economy by exercising broad powers to set prices and wages. For laissez-faire capitalists like Napoleon Hill, the concept smacked of socialism, and some even compared it to Mussolini's brand of fascism in Italy. But the NRA's greatest challenge—indeed, its purpose for being—was to inspire confidence and vitality among American citizens. Hill, one of the very few private citizens who had been quixotic enough to attempt this very thing on his own, was a natural for the position. He signed on at once. And, like his stint with the Wilson administration during World War I, he refused a salary.

CHAPTER 6

1933–1941

THE WHITE HOUSE
April 24, 1933

My dear Mr. Hill:

The President has asked me to thank you for your letter of April twentieth. He appreciates your kindness in letting him know of the sentiment you have found in your contact with the public. He wishes to talk to you about this at the Saturday conference.

> Sincerely,
> LOUIS McH. HOWE
> Secretary to the President

Napoleon Hill's personal record of his relationship with Franklin Delano Roosevelt and FDR's administration was surprisingly scant. In conversations with close friends and in some of his papers, Hill sometimes claimed to have coined the historic remark, "We have nothing to fear but fear itself," and to have written a number of Roosevelt's "fireside chats."

As unlikely as that may have seemed to Hill's many critics and enemies, the least likely proposition of all was that the aristocratic, ultraliberal Roosevelt and the self-taught arch-conservative Hill would find in each other a trusted and valued partner in the struggle to change America's fortunes.

Looked at through another set of eyes, however, this partnership—Hill called it a Master Mind Alliance—was a logical union of two men who felt that the overriding issue of the day was to restore public confidence in the American system. Hill had spent several years trying to stem the tide of the depression on his own, preaching the gospel of what W. Clement Stone would later call a positive mental attitude to businesspeople and private citizens alike. Roosevelt faced the same challenge from a higher pulpit and recognized the fact that in this struggle, the art of verbal persuasion—the ability to change people's minds with the spoken and written word—was at least as important as legislation. In 1933 America, Napoleon Hill had few peers as a spellbinding orator, and no one except perhaps Roosevelt himself could match Hill's ability to articulate a philosophy to all levels of American society.

Thus early in 1933, shortly after Roosevelt took office, the White House secretary called Hill early one morning to ask Napoleon to meet with the president. Hill arrived for the meeting within the hour and the two men quickly came to terms. Roosevelt wanted to supplement the government's traditional public-information apparatus with some decidedly untraditional approaches to shaping public opinion. Hill's role: to listen to and report on the mood of grassroots America, to offer ideas for effective communication with grassroots America, and to oversee a number of different projects designed to overcome Americans' doubts and fears.

"Nothing was said about the compensation I would receive or who would pay it," Hill wrote in *The Science of Personal Achievement,* a book written years later. "I was not thinking of what I might get. I was more concerned with what I might give to help the President antidote the deluge of fear which had spread throughout the country."

Hill's first assignment was to identify every conceivable institution that affected public opinion in America and to outline strategies for enlisting these institutions in the war on fear. Hill's prodigious response covered the obvious—Congress and the media—as well as previously overlooked but incredibly powerful institutions such as public schools and religious leaders.

The administration wasted no time converting Hill's ideas into an action plan, and Hill conceded nothing to modesty in assessing the effectiveness of the program:

> When it was finished, the President of the United States had at his command one of the most powerful master-mind creations this country has ever set into motion.
>
> The plan provided for a crossing of party lines in both Houses of Congress. . . .
>
> The plan provided for the mobilization of the clergy of all denominations. And what a masterful job the churches did from the pulpit in selling the United States back to the people who had been temporarily overcome with fear. I had never seen anything like this before nor have I done so since.
>
> The newspapers and radio stations were brought into the master-mind orbit. Very soon the scare headlines about "Business Depression" were replaced with headlines announcing rapid "Business Recovery."
>
> The public schools at all levels were brought into the gigantic public opinion creative setup which the President had put into action. Through the teachers the students began to hear some of the fine things about their country

which had been overlooked by the peddlers of fear and mistrust.

Roosevelt's famous "fireside chats" were a natural supplement to the administration's broad-based assault on defeatism. As one of FDR's conduits to the grassroots citizenry, Hill supplied the president with a steady stream of suggestions for topics. And, fully aware of his own powers of persuasion, Hill was never bashful about supplying a script that would help the president make his point.

Hill won admiration and warm appreciation from Roosevelt and the White House staff for his selfless dedication, but he had to endure his full share of good-natured ribbing, too. One of Hill's favorite anecdotes from that period focused on the salary negotiations that finally took place several months after he began working for FDR.

One day the President asked me how much I was being paid and who was paying it. "I would like to know this also," I replied.

We discussed the matter for a few seconds without reaching any decision. Then I said, "Mr. President, I didn't accept this assignment with the thought of being paid for it, so let's just put me on the payroll for one dollar per year."

Steve Early, the President's Press Secretary, was sitting in on the conversation. When I mentioned the dollar per year, Steve said, "Alright Nap, the Sap, if that is all you ask for that will be all you get."

From that day forward, President Roosevelt and Steve Early always addressed me as "Nap, the Sap." A part of my job was to deliver speeches on behalf of the President, before business groups throughout the nation. At one of these meetings in Cumberland, Maryland, a member of the

President's staff introduced me as "Nap, the Sap," then explained how I got the moniker. The crowd yelled and I blushed.

Alas, to Florence Hill and the boys, Napoleon's patriotic largesse was neither humorous nor heroic. It was the final blow to a marriage and family relationship that had always come second to Napoleon's evangelistic obsessions. Napoleon was barely able to support himself with writing and lecturing activities during this period, leaving Florence and the boys to fend for themselves, as was so often the case. They did. Indeed, using their own initiative and with support from Florence's family and Napoleon's father, all three boys attended college, and David and Blair graduated.

But their grim struggle in those cheerless economic times created swelling waves of bitterness and resentment toward Napoleon, not just from Florence's family but from Florence herself, from his own father, and even from his sons, one of whom—Jimmie—had been adopted by Florence's brother.

Letters and visits between Napoleon and his wife and sons became less and less frequent during the depression years. A 1934 letter from Nap to David, then a student at Berea Academy in Kentucky, reflected the somber estrangement that had evolved between the struggling father and his family: "It was good to be with all of you boys during the Christmas holidays, a pleasure I had not anticipated until your mother came after me at Martinsburg," wrote Napoleon. "There were some things about the visit that left a sort of unhappy feeling, but on the whole I was glad to have my three fine boys together for a few days once more. It seems that conditions have been such that I could not be much of a father to you, but you have been mighty fortunate just the same, because your mother has been mother and father both. . . ."

Later in the same letter, Hill added, "I wish you would

write to me as well as to your mother. After all, I am your father, you know, and I do get lonesome for news from my boys, although Blair is very good about keeping me informed of his and Jimmie's affairs generally."

In the summer of 1934, Napoleon returned to Lumberport and took Florence and his sons to Chicago for the World's Fair. The excursion proved to be a bittersweet farewell. "It was," recalled David Hill, "the last time we went anywhere together."

In 1935, Florence finally severed the marital ties altogether with help from Napoleon's father. Since divorce was not legal in West Virginia then, James Hill, completely sympathetic to Florence's plight, paid for her to take a trip to Florida, where she won an uncontested divorce. James and Napoleon rarely spoke or wrote to each other again after that time, though Napoleon's parents continued their relationship with Florence and the boys for the rest of their lives.

Napoleon bore his own bitter scars from the divorce. From that point forth, his references to his childhood invoked images of poverty, illiteracy, ignorance, and subhuman darkness. The sole ray of light that would ever pierce this picture was his stepmother, Martha Hill. Even on those rare occasions when he alluded to his father's remarkable path to dentistry and success, the references were terse and all credit for James's accomplishments was accorded Martha. Similarly, in his private journal he rationalized his divorce as something that had been inevitable from the early days of the marriage, due to Florence's lack of focus. Perhaps within himself Napoleon realized that this was a purely self-serving criticism because, to his credit, he never published that passage nor spoke of it in public.

Napoleon was fifty years old when the divorce was finalized. He spent the next two years working for the Roosevelt administration and scratching out a living as best he could. Though virtually all of his income came from writing and lecturing, he continued the futile effort to make something out of his International Publishing Corporation. By 1934, convinced finally that there was no money to be made selling books, he changed the company's focus to that of an ersatz charitable organization engaged in helping people succeed—and proceeded to solicit contributions from shareholders. The effort produced very little revenue, but it did inspire Napoleon to create monumentally clever direct-mail solicitations. In one such letter, he began by equating the principle of a "pleasing personality" with demonstrating interest in others.

Your company is endeavoring to build such a personality here by taking an interest in the problems of others, and endeavoring to help them solve same by introducing them to the *Laws of Success.*

I am sure if you could see the grateful letters we receive from many whom have been helped, you would realize the real service you, as a loyal shareholder, can help carry forward here and [you would] appreciate the great reward which the 'Old Sound Law of Compensation' should bring you for every sacrifice you make in helping us to help others.

The law of increasing returns has proved seed planted in fertile soil will return to you multiplied manifold, therefore, it should be to your advantage to plant the largest number possible of these seeds.

You can . . . get on our honor roll for this month [and] help us continue our sound step by step building program of making each month surpass the preceding one by mailing us the largest possible remittance today on your signed pledge.

Forward yours at once realizing the seed you are planting by helping us help others should bring you a great har-

vest. . . . We are counting on you. REMEMBER, WE
CAN DO IT AND ONLY WE CAN DO IT.

Writing, lecturing, and consulting to FDR kept Hill busy,
but not busy enough. To cope with his postmarital isolation,
he found it necessary to work himself to exhaustion. Thus, to
fill many long, lonely nights, he labored over several different
manuscripts in preparation for the day Americans would
once again dare to dream of success and to pursue it.

Toward the end of 1936, Napoleon's work with the Roosevelt administration was winding down and the national
economy was beginning to eke upward. Audiences for his
lectures swelled in number—he was, after all, a high-profile
presidential adviser—and his ability to seize the hearts and
souls of large groups of people produced thunderous
applause. Demand for his oratory grew, and soon he was on
the lecture tour again, bringing his spine-tingling oratory of
success to podiums all over the country.

While Hill thrilled to the rapt attention of his audiences
and the electric emotion that crackled in the air during his
delivery, he found life on the road in a never-ending succession of cities and towns a desperately lonely proposition,
especially for a man with no wife to write to. He began as a
matter of course to scan his audience as he spoke, looking for
attractive, single women that might fulfill his vision of the
perfect wife. Once, in Knoxville, Tennessee, he set aside his
prepared remarks and abruptly announced to an audience
that his greatest aim in life was to find his "dream girl"—and
then he proceeded to describe her.

Given Napoleon's public stature and his ability to win the
adulation of an audience, his open interest in and availability
to unattached women undoubtedly produced a rich variety
of volunteers. While few could hope to meet Hill's lofty mar-

ital standards, according to his friends and confidants, Napoleon was, by this time in his life, fully prepared to enjoy the opportunities for companionship, in all its variety.

As a man looking for love, Napoleon's pulse probably pounded a little harder some time later when he stepped to the podium in Atlanta to address an audience of nearly one hundred women. As Nap launched into his lecture he also began his habitual evaluation of interesting faces in the crowd. There were many, but none so striking as the twenty-nine-year-old woman who was briefly introduced to him just before the lecture began. Her name was Rosa Lee Beeland, and she recounted their first meeting several years later in her book *How to Attract Men and Money:* "He looked me over with a sweep of his eyes which went from my head to my feet and back again, then bowed and walked quickly away. I learned later that he scratched me from his 'suspect' list at first glance because he thought I had 'too much good looks and too little brains.' "

Whatever doubts Nap really had about Rosa Lee's intellect and suitability for marriage at the time of their introduction were swept aside by her dazzling beauty and steamy sex appeal when they met again after the lecture.

Although he never admitted it, Hill may have been plotting a second meeting with Rosa Lee when he concluded his lecture by offering to meet privately with any student who wished to consult him about their personal problems. Whatever Nap's motivation, he provided just the opportunity Rosa Lee was looking for. She had decided midway through the lecture that she wanted to marry Napoleon Hill, and she patiently waited to be his last interview so she could have all the time she needed to get things moving in the right direction.

As it turned out, Rosa Lee had the mighty Napoleon Hill's heart doing flip-flops in a matter of minutes. They had hardly begun talking when he was smitten by the realization that this was the "dream girl" he had conceived in his own mind. In the next moment, like schoolboys through time immemorial, Nap's knees turned to jelly and his head turned to mush.

"His face suddenly turned white as a sheet," recalled Rosa Lee. "He began to fidget around like someone who was ill. He got up and pranced around the room, went back and sat down in a seat somewhat nearer me. He got up again, pranced around some more, then sat down again. His mind obviously was not upon the question of finding and solving my personal problems. Finally, he arose and announced the interview was to be postponed until the following afternoon."

That night Rosa Lee vented her indignation at Hill's brusk treatment of her to a friend, but she showed up for their interview the next day. By then Nap had pulled himself together. Before they even sat down he explained his earlier conduct as that of a lovestruck man, then told her why the emotion had so overwhelmed him. They talked for five hours and left the room engaged. Weeks later, they were married.

In her book, Rosa Lee attributed their whirlwind courtship and marital bliss to the "great universal law of Harmonious Attraction." For Hill, "harmonious attraction" was a circumspect expression for the tides of lust that Rosa Lee aroused in him. For Rosa Lee, it probably covered a broader swath of life.

Rosa Lee's mother died in childbirth, leaving her to be raised by her father and an aunt. One of the enduring lessons of her childhood was her father's advice to try to please herself rather than engage in the futility of pleasing others. By her own account, Rosa Lee quickly developed into an independent, strong-willed girl who, at the age of fifteen, began planning how to attract the *right* man. By the time she and Napoleon met, she not only knew what kind of man she wanted to marry, she was also prepared to wait as long as it took to find what she wanted.

Rosa Lee's book suggested that marrying for wealth was as honorable as any other motive—and far more practical. However, her attraction to Nap was probably based more on intrigue than imminent riches. He was flat broke and had no immediate prospects for quick success. On the other hand, he was famous, connected to the most powerful men in government and business, and, because of his age and cocksure personality, offered a father figure–like sense of security.

They married early in 1937, just as the last of Nap's money ran out. Napoleon's son Blair, the one member of the family who remained blindly loving and loyal to him, came to their rescue. Blair and his own new bride had set up housekeeping in a tiny apartment in New York's infamous Hell's Kitchen neighborhood, and they opened their home to Napoleon and Rosa Lee.

The arrangement was an utter disaster for Blair and his wife. The cramped quarters made privacy nearly impossible, and Blair was immediately put off by his father's lusty attentions to another woman. Soon, the problem was exacerbated as he found that, his loyalties to Florence aside, there was nothing to like about Rosa Lee. But by far and away the foursome's most severe and unrelenting source of misery was Napoleon himself. He managed to drive everyone crazy. He lectured Blair endlessly about how to succeed and hounded him night and day about his cigarette smoking; indeed, in his private journal, Nap devoted more than twenty manuscript pages of nerve-wracking rantings about Blair's "filthy" vice. But no one suffered more from Napoleon's presence than Blair's wife, Vera. She bore the full brunt of Napoleon's ability to unashamedly heckle and hound people he didn't like. Vera endured several months of Nap's nastiest bullying and sniping, then finally left Blair and moved back to West Virginia. Blair soon returned to West Virginia too, after loaning his father enough money to subsist for several more months. Blair and Vera tried to rebuild their marriage but several years later were divorced. Although Blair went on to become an eminently successful businessman and a beloved community leader, he never remarried.

Napoleon's vitriolic attacks probably stemmed from the pent-up frustrations he felt, not only from his living situation but also from the tensions of writing and marketing a new book. Day and night he worked over one of the manuscripts written during his years in FDR's service. And, whatever her other shortcomings might have been, Rosa Lee worked with him and turned out to be the exacting editor he had been missing since Don Mellet's assassination. Rosa Lee typed every page of every draft of the manuscript. Along the way she challenged him to streamline and clarify disjointed thoughts, to cut entire passages in which he wandered too far from his theme, to rewrite paragraphs, pages, and even entire chapters until his thoughts were clearly and concisely expressed.

The completed manuscript, entitled *The Thirteen Steps to Riches,* was rewritten three times before they showed it to Andrew Pelton, Hill's publisher. And Rosa Lee had shown Napoleon that she could maintain his twenty-hour-a-day pace without complaint. "By the time she had finished the manuscript on the third re-write," recalled Napoleon, "the tips of her fingers were so worn and blistered she had to tape them so she could work . . . but she was so enthusiastic . . . that she said it was a pleasure to wear her fingers to the bone in such a labor of love."

After weeks of sleepless toil, Hill invited Andrew Pelton to the apartment and presented the manuscript to him. The publisher read the table of contents and thumbed through a few pages of text, then gave the eager Hills his verdict: It was just another self-help book, essentially the same as Hill's previous work and several other titles that he had published in recent years and which were not selling.

Despite the torture the Hills had endured to produce the manuscript, they received the publisher's sentiments with surprising aplomb. "We knew before he ever saw the manuscript that he was going to publish it," explained Hill. "We gave that matter no concern whatsoever. . . .

"After he had talked all afternoon analyzing the book and trying to prove to us it was not very different from other books . . . my wife suggested that he take the manuscript home with him, read it, and then he would know what was in it that was not in my previous books or in any other book he had published."

Rosa Lee was nothing if not persuasive with men, and Pelton assented. Three days later he appeared at their apartment once more, ready to take a chance on the book on one condition—that the title be changed to something more catchy.

In the lore surrounding this particular publishing venture, one story suggested that right up to the eve of the first printing the publisher wanted to call it *Use Your Noodle to Win More Boodle*. In the end, however, the book was published under the title *Think and Grow Rich!*, and its fame and popularity would begin immediately and last through the rest of the century.

Andrew Pelton had every right to be reluctant to invest in an inspirational self-help book that spoke of riches and success in 1937 America. Although the New Deal had succeeded in getting the economy moving forward again, the pace of improvement was agonizingly slow. Millions of Americans were still out of work and millions more were underemployed. America's Great Depression was showing only the slightest glimmerings of dissipating; it would, in fact, extend through the remainder of the decade. There was no tangible reason to believe that Nap's new title would have any more appeal to a tattered and besieged nation than *The Magic Ladder to Success* created in the early thirties.

Playing his own gut hunch, Pelton not only printed *Think and Grow Rich!*, he also slapped a $2.50 retail price on it and ordered five thousand copies in the first pressrun—a fairly optimistic quantity for the day.

Incredibly, that seemingly risky print order turned out to be woefully inadequate for the demand. Three weeks after the book went into distribution, the entire print run was sold out. There followed an endless succession of printings and larger print orders as the book became a huge best-seller. If anyone in America was looking for a tangible sign that private citizens were shaking off the mental and emotional stigma of the depression, *Think and Grow Rich!* provided it in hard sales figures. Shortly after its initial appearance, one insurance company purchased five thousand copies of the book in a single order. Tens of thousands more were purchased in other bulk orders, while hundreds of thousands of single-copy sales were being rung up in direct mail and retail store offerings.

Well over a million copies of the book were sold even before the depression lifted, and it would continue to sell in large volume for decades and generations to come—all over America and throughout the world. Ten years later, *Think and Grow Rich!* ranked fourth in a leading magazine's poll on books that most influenced the lives of the successful men of the forties. Fifty years later, the twenty-millionth copy of the book was sold; it remained an active title in thousands of libraries and was still stocked by leading bookstores throughout the country.

Why would a book once thought to be like any other succeed on such a grand scale?

The answer probably stems from the fact that the content

of *Think and Grow Rich!* originated from *Law of Success* and Hill's unique Carnegie-inspired, twenty-year investigation of what makes people succeed. The research itself, and the content of *Law of Success,* are among the most original works in modern American publishing.

No doubt much of the publisher's initial objection to *Think and Grow Rich!* was the fact that most of its concepts were drawn from Hill's discussion of the principles of success in his earlier book. Unlike *Law of Success,* however, the new publication was written as a book, not a collection of lecture notes. Its focus was practical information that the reader could apply directly to his or her own situation, while *Law of Success* was part philosophical treatise, part textbook. And most of all, where *Law of Success* twisted and turned along the oft circuitous trail of its undisciplined author's philosophical discourses, *Think and Grow Rich!* presented its blend of anecdotes, facts, checklists, and advice in a lean and clear style that merchandised Hill's inspirational genius to a large cross section of the reading public.

While Rosa Lee's work is thought to have influenced the clarity and conciseness of *Think and Grow Rich!,* the book also demonstrated an infinitely more mature and sophisticated Napoleon Hill. Concepts such as dealing with one's own sex drive that had been covered vaguely in earlier works were presented with logic and authentic research in the new book. Other concepts, like imagination, had been refined to new levels of usefulness. Hill was one of the first to link imagination to success in business; in *Think and Grow Rich!* he set forth a distinction between "synthetic" and "creative" imagination; the distinction, and his advice on how to cultivate and employ both qualities, remained valid and instructive four decades later when creativity became the subject of scientific research and a prized goal of educational and business institutions.

Think and Grow Rich! set forth thirteen "steps to riches," each a chapter in its own right. The "steps" ranged from such traditional fare as desire and faith, to more avant-garde concepts like Auto-Suggestion (tapping the subconscious mind), the "Mystery of Sex Transmutation" (how to satisfy your sexual urges and also employ them in a career), and "The Brain" (the pragmatic lessons of telepathy). Most chapters included punchy self-help lists summarizing five- or six-point action plans that the reader could immediately apply to his or her own life. The chapter on Organized Planning included a half-dozen such templates, each of which was still embraced by legions of management and business consultants five decades later.

The book was practical and readable. It informed and advised and, perhaps more important, it inspired readers to think, to take inventory of themselves and their times, to consider options, to apply imagination and creativity to plotting a direction for their lives. But *Think and Grow Rich!* had another quality as well, one that helped keep it fresh and original through its long-running success. One critic put it best: "Far more than a schematic for attaining financial success, *Think and Grow Rich!* was suffused with a spirituality that transcended religious doctrine, that evoked the innate goodness in people, the extraordinariness in all of us, and promised that if we nurtured these precious gifts and used them wisely, we would enhance not only our own lives but the lives of everyone we meet."

It was those very qualities of *Think and Grow Rich!* that caught the eye of an obscure Chicago insurance salesman in 1938. W. Clement Stone had received a copy of Hill's hot-selling book as a gift from a sales consultant who was trying to get Stone to purchase his services. Stone was not much of a prospect for anything that cost money at that time. After a promising start, his insurance agency had been devastated by the depression. When *Think and Grow Rich!* was placed on his desk, Stone had pared his sales force down to a skeletal group of 135 and was still nearly thirty thousand dollars in debt.

Although Stone had never heard of Hill or his famous best-seller before, the title piqued his curiosity and he opened it up. As he flipped through the pages, Stone became more and more interested in what Hill had to say and finally read the book from cover to cover. He found that Hill's philosophy was very similar to his own and that the book gave him new insights that he could apply to his own business. One of those insights was the Master Mind principle—people working in harmony toward a common goal.

"I had had some concern over hiring men in my office," Stone explained later. "I thought that perhaps some might later become my competitors. The Master Mind principle made me realize that I could multiply my efforts by employing others—individuals of good character—to do much of the work that I was doing or couldn't take the time to do."

Stone was so enthusiastic about the book's blend of inspiration and practical advice that he provided copies of it to every one of his salesmen. "Fantastic things began to happen," he recalled. "Many of my salesmen became super salesmen. Sales and profits increased. Their attitudes had changed from negative to positive. Those who were searching for the secret of success realized that they . . . had unlimited potential powers to affect their subconscious minds through the conscious."

By 1939, in part because of the impact *Think and Grow Rich!* had on him personally and on his salesmen, Stone's sales force had swelled to more than one thousand, his company had soared beyond even its predepression peak, and Stone himself was blazing a trail of success that would ultimately rival the likes of Carnegie and Edison.

It seemed that not even the free-spending Napoleon Hill could make a dent in the wealth that poured down on him and Rosa Lee as *Think and Grow Rich!* swept through America. Their hand-to-mouth poverty was almost instantly washed away as the bulging royalty checks began rolling in. A year later they could account their net worth in tens of thousands of dollars, and their royalties would continue to multiply. By 1940 Hill claimed to be worth more than a million dollars.

While fragmentary financial records suggest that Hill's fortune fell well short of a million dollars, he was suddenly far wealthier than he had ever imagined he would be. One book had netted Hill more money in two years than he had made in any previous ten-year period of his life. One book, created in the earliest months of their marriage, had transformed the distinguished but penniless man Rosa Lee pursued into a rich and influential public personality. One book born of their combined tireless labors, mental anguish, and physical discomfort had, overnight almost, given Rosa Lee more wealth and status than she had ever dreamed possible.

And it changed them both.

At first, it was merely appearances. Ever the fashion-conscious dandy, Napoleon filled his closets with expensive suits from exclusive tailors—and applauded gaily as Rosa Lee accumulated her own endless variety of delectable fashions, each exquisite piece in perfect taste and each perfectly designed to compliment her trim figure and stylish coiffures. With the wardrobes came expensive cars, high-brow restaurants, a prestigious address.

But somewhere in the rush of gilded trinkets and public acclaim, each of them in their own way began to shrivel into a smaller, more cynical person. With all his riches, Napoleon never thought to pay back his favorite son for the loan that made the writing of *Think and Grow Rich!* possible. Rosa Lee was even more insufferable, at least when it came to Blair and the rest of Napoleon's family. None of this went unnoticed by Blair, who wrote in a letter to Florence in early 1938,

"Golly, when I think back over the past recent months—I don't see how I could have been taken in so, as I was by Father. When I needed assistance, YOU came to bat for me—not he! . . .

". . . Father's wife wrote me a letter . . . which I feel she wrote to taunt me with the fact that 'the Gods have been good to them,' and 'they can retire now.' Meaning that had I allowed Father to ride roughshod over me and Vera, we'd be on top financially with them. . . .

". . . To this letter I wrote a reply, stating in sum and substance that if she were really my friend as she professed in the letter, then to prove it by remembering their promises to repay me when they were able—by sending me $300 so I could pay off my bills and have enough to get along on for awhile."

Blair, who had spent his life adoring and apologizing for his father to the rest of the family, had finally had enough. In the same letter, he described his father as an "unscrupulous, holier-than-thou, two-timing, double crossing good-for-nothing."

"Sometime," Blair vowed, "I'm going to see that he pays and pays plenty for the way he treated you, treated me, treated David and Jimmy!"

But Blair was not a vengeful sort and would never inflict pain on his father. And, even had he tried, he could never have done to Napoleon what Rosa Lee and Napoleon himself would soon manage to do.

While Rosa Lee basked in the glory of her own fame, extolling the wonders of her fairy-tale marriage in public appearances and private interviews, Napoleon was back on the road with a lecture series. Somewhere along the way, Rosa Lee began to suspect that he was spending his non-speaking hours in the company of other women. Whether Rosa Lee's suspicions were roused by rumors, fact, or sheer jealousy will never be known.

What is certain is that by 1940, the Hills and their marriage were a sham. Rosa Lee's book *How to Attract Men and
Money* was published that year. It was in part a tribute to the
Hills' loftiest expectations for their own marriage, but it
would finally prove to be nothing more than a chronicle of
shattered dreams.

The book was an inventive exploitation of *Think and
Grow Rich!* and Hill's philosophy. Its subtitle boldly promised,
"A new philosophy of proven methods that will help single
women find and marry the right man ... and enable all
women to inspire the men of their choice to achieve greater
financial success." Part of the book's premise was that Rosa
Lee had achieved a fairy-tale life as a princess in a Florida castle all because she had applied the philosophies of business
success to the business of attracting men, picking the right
one, and making him rich. The book opened with photos of
the Hills' pretentious home, a replicated castle overlooking
Lake Dora, Florida. The impressive structure was identified in
the caption as Castle-on-the-Hill, the "residence and literary
workshop of Mr. and Mrs. Napoleon Hill."

In her introduction to the main text, Rosa Lee told of her
passion for children and how she and Napoleon were enriching the world by sharing their home and lives with fifteen
adopted kids:

> I live in a beautiful mansion, located in Florida, on a
> high rolling hill of many acres covered by beautiful trees,
> overlooking a gorgeous lake which gives us miles of unob-
> structed vision.

> Here my husband and I maintain what we believe to be
> the most unique home in all the world. We are adopting
> and rearing 15 boys and girls. We are proving, through
> these children, that there is nothing wrong with the

younger generation except their parents, some of their teachers and many adults whom they are trying to ape.

Our family is not yet complete, but we have gone far enough with our experiment to feel confident we can send our children back to the world from which we took them, fully prepared to encounter and master all the evils of the day, and to master all chances of economic distress.

Outside of our home our wards are submitted to all the usual in harmonies among people; inside our home they never feel the influence of a single negative word.

The Hills and their publisher may have felt this image of a domestic utopia was important to the acceptance of a book that otherwise offered a rich diet of materialistic propositions about how women should live their lives, select their mates, and run their marriages. The cornerstone of Rosa Lee's philosophy was, if you're going to go to all the trouble of finding the *right* man, he might as well be a rich one.

Similarly, *How to Attract Men and Money* offered many passages written by both Rosa Lee and Napoleon about marital love, dedication, openness, and trust. "We have no family secrets," wrote Rosa Lee. "The mail is placed on the office table in the morning and it is read aloud by one of us."

Later, in a section written by Napoleon, he stated, "My wife has no fear of ever losing me; she has no concern over my becoming interested in other women; she has no concern over anything connected with her relationship with me save only that of remaining always harmonious with me. . . . In our relationship there is no room for jealousy, envy or other destructive influences because our minds are completely filled with positive thought and we are therefore constantly engaged in constructive deeds."

Napoleon and Rosa Lee apparently started out with a

sincere desire to fulfill the divine visions they painted of their lives and their marriage in Rosa Lee's book. When they moved into their Mount Dora castle in 1939, Napoleon's income tax records show that they claimed two adopted dependents. However, it is not clear how long the two children actually lived in the Hill home, nor what became of them. What is certain is that the Hills' plans for rearing a large brood of children were a distant and hollow memory by the time *How to Attract Men and Money* was in distribution. So was their marital trust and their economic ease.

The financial stress came first. It began with the purchase of the Mount Dora estate in 1939, which offered Napoleon and Rosa Lee the residential splendor befitting a millionaire couple. Unfortunately, though they were wealthy, and though Napoleon often liked to promote himself as a millionaire author and philosopher, they were not millionaires and could not afford the sumptuous dwelling and the hired help it took to care for the place. Hill later claimed, bitterly, that the estate was Rosa Lee's idea—and it probably was. But it made an excellent parking place for Nap's own contribution to the couple's financial straits, an immaculately maintained Rolls-Royce.

By mid-1939, the Hills were on the verge of insolvency. In a desperate attempt to raise more cash, Napoleon packed his bags and went to New York City to lecture, write, and try to negotiate a book contract with an advance large enough to keep them afloat.

According to Napoleon, early in 1940, Rosa Lee came to New York and convinced him to sell two years of future royalties to Pelton for five thousand dollars. It was a deal born of a desperate need for immediate cash, for two years of Hill's royalties were worth three or four times the amount they got. On the other hand, if that was what Rosa Lee wanted, there wasn't much Hill could do about it—he had signed over to her virtually all royalties to all his books in a 1937 premarital contract. The contract was designed to shield Napoleon's earnings from claims brought by his previous associates, debt holders, or Florence, but in the financial difficulties of 1939 and 1940, it became a weapon in his own destruction.

Unbeknownst to Napoleon, Rosa Lee had also retained the services of an attorney in Mount Dora. Initially, she may have consulted the lawyer for advice on how to save the Hills' crumbling financial empire, but the legal advice quickly turned to planning a divorce.

The end to the marriage of Rosa Lee and Napoleon Hill came quickly and with ruthless destruction. After Napoleon gave her the royalty money from Pelton, Rosa Lee returned to Mount Dora and sold everything the couple owned, including Nap's beloved Rolls.

Years later, Napoleon recounted what happened next in a letter to a New York attorney: "I left New York in May 1940 and went to Atlanta, Georgia where I began a radio program in an attempt to re-establish myself financially. While in Atlanta I lived with [Rosa Lee's] aunts who, incidentally, were greatly disturbed by her actions which had led to my financial disaster. While living there, about the middle of the year 1940, my former wife telephoned me that she was filing for a divorce and threatened to have me arrested for non support if I did not sign a waiver and give her the divorce without opposition."

According to Hill, he was subsequently coerced by Rosa Lee and her attorney to employ an Atlanta attorney of their choice to represent him in the matter. At that point, however, no coercion was necessary for Rosa Lee to get what she wanted. Armed with a premarital agreement which essentially gave her the rights to everything he had ever written or would write during their marriage, Rosa Lee was assured of an overwhelmingly generous property settlement. Hill's best defense might have been to fight the divorce itself, but his

reputation would have been brutally assaulted in the pro-
ceedings and he had little chance of winning. Worse yet, had
he won he would still have been married to Rosa Lee.

Shocked, humiliated, and defeated, Napoleon acquiesced
to Rosa Lee's every demand. The uncontested property settlement was filed in January 1941, and the final decree followed in March. Less than a year after *How to Attract Men and
Money* rolled off the presses carrying Rosa Lee's proclamation
that she and Napoleon were "two people who have made
married life a paradise of happiness," Rosa Lee took possession of every asset Hill had and sent him on his way—a fifty-
six-year-old pauper.

The final humiliation of Napoleon Hill came after the
divorce, and it was packaged in bitter layers of irony.

It was widely assumed among the couple's friends and
associates that the Hills' divorce was the result of philander-
ing on the part of Napoleon. Rosa Lee let it be known that
she had suspected him of indiscretions and had hired a private detective to follow him in the later months of their marriage. Napoleon's guilt or innocence on this score is a matter
of pure speculation—although he confessed publicly to many
embarrassing flaws, faults, and mistakes in judgment, he never
listed infidelity as one of his failings, never spoke of it to his
closest confidants, and did not impress his friends and family
as a man who would engage in extramarital activities.

Rosa Lee, on the other hand, blazed a trail of doubt about
her own purity by marrying her attorney shortly after her
divorce from Napoleon was finalized. Napoleon, for one,
concluded that he had been cuckolded, and that Rosa Lee
and her attorney had conspired to ruin him as a way of sub-
sidizing their love affair.

Apparently things didn't turn out any better in Rosa Lee's
second marriage than they had in her first. After he surmised
what had happened, Napoleon tried to track down Rosa Lee

for subsequent legal action. When he finally located her in 1944 she had sold her royalty rights to Pelton—reportedly for a pittance—and was serving in the military under her maiden name. After the war she disappeared again until resurfacing briefly in 1950 to take a quick stab at suing Hill's agent for two thousand dollars in back royalties. It was a fruitless and perhaps desperate lawsuit—the agent turned the matter over to Hill, who was prepared and eager for another legal showdown . . . and Rosa Lee sank out of sight.

Perhaps the final humiliation in 1941 helped Napoleon get back on his feet. Despite his initial devastation over the divorce and the prospect of starting over again at the seemingly advanced age of fifty-six, Hill soon began laying plans for the future with his customary enthusiasm. He had been through so many boom-and-bust cycles by then, and had accumulated so many fond memories of the periods of his life spent rebuilding from hopeless disasters, perhaps he was being completely candid when he told his friends, "I walked out of that marriage with nothing but the shirt on my back and my battered old typewriter. I lost everything. Millions. But it was worth it just to be rid of her."

CHAPTER 7

1941-1951

As the specter of Nazi Germany cast its nightmare pall over Europe, Hill suffered through the last days of 1940 in a personal purgatory. Financial destitution was one shock, but that trauma passed quickly. Hill had played that hand many times before and knew he could make a good living. What struck deep inside and stayed with him was the spirit-numbing agony of isolation. For the first time since he began courting Florence more than twenty years before, he felt completely and utterly alone. His father was dead, his sons would not speak to him. There was no woman to offer him solace and support, nor even to provide an audience for his expressions of pain.

During these cheerless days, Napoleon overcame his pride and went to Florence hat-in-hand to ask for a reconciliation. Solid, steady, resourceful Florence had been the one constant in so many of his years of turbulence. But Florence would have none of it. Having raised and educated three boys by herself through the worst and longest economic depression in American history, Florence was enjoying a modest but comfortable life in Florida. Her appetite for Napoleon's roller-coaster life had long since been sated. Her answer was an irrevocable No.

Hill passed the Christmas of 1940 in joyless solitude. He took his meals alone in the sparsely occupied restaurant of his unpretentious hotel. He spent the day reading newspaper accounts of Hitler's European expansionism, the debate over U.S. involvement in "Europe's war," and the latest successes and failures of the New Deal. There were no gifts to be opened, precious few cards to be read.

Christmas dissolved into an empty succession of days and nights, and then a silent New Year's, and then the holidays were thankfully gone. Hill knew through a lifetime of experience, no matter how much his depression resisted the notion, that it was time to get moving again. And he did.

The mid-winter sky hung low and dark over the deep forests of western South Carolina as Napoleon made his way along the quiet two-lane highway. He drove through the hushed landscape and failing light with a practiced precision, staying at the posted speed limit, watchful for deer, alert for the occasional oncoming motorist, ever attentive to his own driving. His car was a late-model DeSoto coupe. It was no Rolls-Royce, to be sure, but with its long hood, arching fenders, and rakish deck, the DeSoto's sporty flair turned heads on the road and made a clear statement about the man at the wheel: Neither age nor divorce had robbed Napoleon Hill of the panache that had powered him out of Appalachia so many years before.

Napoleon was headed north, but this time his destination was not Washington, D.C., or New York or Philadelphia or any of the other great cities he had called home since leaving Wise County. On this somber January afternoon, Hill was picking his way toward Clinton, a bucolic South Carolina town in the gently rolling terrain north of Columbia. With each patient mile his vision of his future began to take focus.

He was far from Florida and Rosa Lee, far from his brief life of glitter and opulence and betrayal, and further still—a lifetime it seemed—from Florence and his sons, from Wise County, and from all else he had been.

By the time Hill pulled into Clinton, he was filled with the tingling sense of adventure that had always been a part of starting over again. Once more, he was stepping into the great unknown. He called it "spinning the wheel of fortune." The only thing he could count on was that the wheel would stop where he'd least expect it—and the chances of plunging from another of life's terrifying cliffs were counterbalanced by the equal chance of catching another soaring star. You had to take your chances to play, and even at the age of fifty-six, Napoleon Hill loved the game too much to content himself with anything less.

At first blush, Clinton, South Carolina, was an unlikely site for Napoleon to choose as a place to start over. Always before he had gravitated toward the great industrial cities of the North, where the opportunities he sought existed in greater abundance than anywhere else. Clinton, in contrast, was a quiet southern town of five thousand people. Two cotton mills owned by one family comprised its main industrial base and helped to justify its railway service. Clinton's other large employer was Dr. William Plumer Jacobs, president of Presbyterian College, owner of Jacobs Press, and public relations counselor to a group of South Carolina textile firms.

It was Jacobs who had drawn Napoleon to Clinton in the January gloom of 1941, and Napoleon would have little trouble finding him. All roads into and out of Clinton led to Broad Street, and Broad Street led to the town center. Jacobs Press commanded a large building just a block from the center.

Napoleon took his first drive down Broad Street at a leisurely pace, soaking in the tranquility of the townscape. Massive oaks spun a leafless canopy overhead. Warm lights were already beginning to glow from the windows of the houses lining the street. The houses themselves were a mixture of elegant Southern traditional architecture and more modest wood-frame dwellings, most immaculately kept, a few neglected. They told Napoleon that Clinton was a moderately prosperous town.

As Napoleon motored slowly through the downtown area, he passed by a monument in the middle of the town center. It was a Civil War monument honoring the soldiers of the Confederate Army. It stirred Hill's memories of growing up in the South, of friends and neighbors with lingering resentment of Sherman's tactics and the prolonged ugly aftermath of the war, with its era of carpetbaggers and corruption. These memories had remained dormant in Napoleon's consciousness for years, but now they would come rushing back inspired not just by the sight of the monument, but especially by the work of William Jacobs.

The deep South of the 1940s was still seen by itself and the rest of the nation as an economically backward region that had never recovered from the Civil War. Much of the greatest American literature of the twentieth century dealt with the crumbling social order and traditions of the old South. It was still an agricultural economy, but labor-intensive farming methods, marginal soil, and a shortage of investment capital had crippled the region's recovery from the Civil War. To many Americans, the South was synonymous with poor schools, rural poverty, and resistance to change.

William Jacobs had a different view of the South, especially of its future. Like many Southern intellectuals, he understood that the region's stunted economic growth stemmed directly from a lack of capital. Southerners were no more or no less resistant to change than anyone else—they simply didn't have the opportunity to change because all the investment capital, all the factories, and all the jobs had remained in the North. When he looked around Georgia and the Carolinas, he saw the poverty and want. But he also saw hard-working people who could perform the same jobs being done in the North by high-paid union workers for less money. He saw in the South's small towns and comparatively small cities ideal locations for Northern businesses—towns that offered competitive highway and rail transportation, a ready supply of water for manufacturing, low taxes, and inexpensive land on which to build factories and offices. He saw a workforce made up of self-reliant, God-fearing men and women whose Puritan work ethic insulated industrialists from strikes and unrest. He believed the South would rise again—economically, this time—by attracting business and industry from the North. And he believed Napoleon Hill could help.

According to Hill, the two men met in an Atlanta restaurant in 1940. Hill was delivering a series of lectures at the restaurant to help the owner, a former Hill student, get his new business off the ground. Jacobs, familiar with Hill's work and perhaps with his radio program, sat in on some of the lectures and arranged to meet privately with Napoleon.

Jacobs's offer to Hill was not a get-rich-quick scheme. It was an opportunity to participate in a noble cause and to get back to his roots as a business evangelist. Hill would relocate to Clinton, rewrite his entire philosophy of personal achievement as a self-help course, and create a lecture series called the Philosophy of American Achievement that would be tested and perfected at Presbyterian College, then delivered in schools, towns, and factories throughout South Carolina and her sister states of the deep South. Hill would also help Jacobs convince a powerful group of Southern business leaders to put up seed money for his pet project: attracting Northern companies to relocate to the South.

Napoleon might well have had more lucrative offers than Jacobs's as 1940 came to a close. But with his marriage to

Rosa Lee coming to a disastrous end and with revelations of her duplicity becoming clear, Hill felt a need to associate with ethical, principled people and to pursue noble goals. Jacobs's offer represented a purity of purpose that, more than money, gave Napoleon a chance to cleanse his soul.

After a quick look around, Hill entered the Jacobs building—and a new life. Jacobs's secretary welcomed him with a gracious smile and announced his arrival to Jacobs. While Jacobs prepared to receive him, Napoleon was introduced to a universally warm office staff, each member of which greeted him with enthusiasm. Clearly, William Jacobs had prepared a royal welcome for his newest associate.

Hill's first meeting in Clinton with Jacobs was direct, brief, and uplifting. As they chatted, Napoleon recounted to Jacobs his reaction when, as a child in Wise County, Virginia, he was taught about General Sherman's scorched-earth march on Atlanta. "It made me so angry that I went into a tantrum," he told Jacobs, "and I vowed that the time would come when I would go up North and do something about those Yankees. . . ."

"Wonderful!" exclaimed Jacobs, with an amused grin. "And tomorrow we will begin doing something about it in earnest."

When their meeting ended, Hill drove a few blocks to the apartment Jacobs provided him to begin settling in. If he harbored any doubts about living in Clinton, they probably disappeared when he pulled into the drive of his new home. The building that housed his apartment was the original home of Jacobs's father, Ferdinand. It was a stately, rambling, three-story structure clad in impeccably trimmed clapboard siding, fronted by a shady porch, and surrounded by an expansive lawn and towering hardwoods. Each floor of the magnificent home had been converted into a large apartment. As the third-floor tenant, Hill had to climb more steps to get home, but it was worth it: When he sat down to his typewriter he could gaze out the window and survey one of the most beautiful landscapes he would ever see. Even as he unpacked, Napoleon's bruised soul began mending.

Hill immediately immersed himself in his work, blending into Clinton's atmosphere of quiet diligence. At first, there were few diversions. His life shuttled between his apartment, Jacobs's offices, and weekly lectures at Presbyterian College. Most of his waking hours were spent pounding away at the typewriter. He methodically reviewed three decades of his own manuscripts, speeches, and letters as well as his dog-eared notes and records of interviews with Carnegie, Edison, Ford, and the other giants who had inspired his works on success . . . sorting out facts and anecdotes, sifting through his life's work to uncover any shreds of material he might previously have overlooked, and challenging his previous interpretations.

All through the day and well into the night the sound of keys tapping in rapid succession streamed from Hill's office and apartment. When he wasn't working on the sixteen-lesson manuscript that would become *Mental Dynamite,* he composed his lectures for Presbyterian College or created letters and literature for Jacobs's campaign to promote industrial growth in the South.

To his neighbors and his associates at Jacobs Press, Napoleon was seen as a quiet, hard-working man. He was congenial and had a good sense of humor, but he was also reserved and very focused on his work. He was never too busy to answer a question about his philosophy or to discuss his current work, but he quickly became known as a man who was simply unable to engage in small talk.

As the weeks and months rolled on, Napoleon thrived in his solitary, near-monastic lifestyle. *Mental Dynamite* progressed rapidly, the Jacobs industrialization project was nearing a climax, and Hill's lectures had become extremely popular, drawing people from miles around. He even found time to compose experimental essays and outline concepts for a philosophical treatise on good and evil in contemporary America.

He was a new man, nearly an alter ego to the "millionaire author" who had achieved notoriety for his womanizing, conceit, and enthusiastic participation in the good life. In Clinton, he was a work-dedicated man who kept largely to himself except in matters of business. The worst that could be said of him was that he enjoyed a good cigar and he refused to participate in organized religion. There was no womanizing, not even dating, and he had no intention of changing that.

Fortunately for Napoleon, however, his romantic intentions weren't the only ones that counted in Clinton in 1941. Unbeknownst to Hill, he had caught the fancy of Annie Lou Norman, Jacobs's secretary. Annie Lou had remained single for forty-seven years, enjoying her gentlemen callers but avoiding the bonds of marriage until a truly worthwhile man might come along. She was a unique blend of Southern tradition and modern pragmatism. She had the charm and grace of a plantation belle, the heart of a social worker, and the no-nonsense business mind of a Carnegie comptroller.

Annie Lou Norman was the second of seven children in a middle-class South Carolina family. The family's passion was education—Annie Lou's father read a great deal and inspired his children to do the same. In early twentieth-century America, when the value of education for males was subject to debate and when education for women was widely considered a waste of time, the elder Norman was a maverick. He taught his children—even his daughters—that the pursuit of knowledge and enlightenment was one of life's highest callings.

His message was not lost on Annie Lou. She soared through primary and secondary education on the wings of a real passion for reading and learning and earned a scholarship to a local college. However, before she could embark on her college career, Annie Lou's father died. As the oldest of the Norman children still living at home, she made the first sacrifice, forsaking college for a job and income vital to the family's welfare.

But fortune did not turn its back entirely on the young Annie Lou. The job she found—indeed, the only job she ever held—was with Jacobs Press, where her love of reading and writing was appreciated and rewarded. At eighteen years of age, she became Ferdinand Jacobs's personal secretary. Intelligent and decisive beyond her years, Annie Lou saw her responsibilities and influence grow rapidly. When William Jacobs took over for his father, Annie Lou knew the company's business inside and out. She could keep the business ledgers, correspond with authors, edit manuscripts, and evaluate submissions.

Annie Lou had plenty of suitors over the years, and while she enjoyed the attention, none of them had the combination of intellect and excitement she sought in a husband. And Annie Lou Norman had no intention of tying herself down to a compromise candidate simply to avoid the "spinster" tag that was applied to middle-aged single women of her day. Annie Lou had her own ideas about what was important in life and what compromises should be made. She dedicated her life to her family and friends, her job, and to her own intellectual pursuits—and enjoyed it all immensely.

Then Napoleon Hill came to town.

Annie Lou Norman had a unique perspective of Clinton's newest resident. As Jacobs's secretary, she was one of the first to meet Hill, and she was thoroughly aware of his literary and philosophical accomplishments, as well as his dynamic business persona.

In addition, Annie Lou had a glimpse of Napoleon's personal life, for she was his neighbor. She lived in the same stately manse that housed Napoleon, sharing the first-floor apartment with her divorced sister, Leila Johnson, and Leila's four-year-old son, Charles. Like Annie Lou, Leila was a well-read working woman employed by Jacobs Press as a proof-reader and shipping clerk.

And, through Leila's eyes, Annie Lou would soon see Napoleon from a third perspective—that of a student. The youngest of the Norman clan, Leila was struggling to make a living—and especially a future—for herself and her young son in the early 1940s. It was a daunting and frustrating chal-lenge. Her ex-husband provided no support, and in pre–World War II America, the business community steered women workers into obscure, low-paying jobs. When Napoleon Hill came to town, Leila Johnson's life was a daily conflict between her dogged determination to provide her son the opportunity to go to college and the aching fear that she would never achieve the professional status and income that achieving her goal would require.

The two sisters attended all of Hill's evening lectures on his philosophy of achievement at Presbyterian College. They walked to the lecture hall together in fair weather and foul (they had no car), and they watched in amazement as their quiet, somewhat shy neighbor ascended to the podium and became another person . . . a supercharged dynamo whose words and thoughts rang through the air in machine-gunfire bursts, filling the hall, mesmerizing the mind, and moving the soul to hope and, finally, action.

For Leila, Napoleon Hill's lectures offered a life-changing opportunity. She was almost immediately a student of the philosophy of success. She would employ Hill's message and his personal counseling to achieve a higher station in her pro-fessional life and to provide for her young son and help him achieve his own lofty goals in life. Inspired by Napoleon's teachings and armed with her own grit and intellect, Leila would persevere through endless nights of study to complete a degree in accounting through a correspondence school . . . and she would see her son Charles become a doctor of medicine.

Hill's lectures were just as stimulating for Annie Lou, but for different reasons. Annie Lou had the tenure and status at Jacobs Press to command a good salary, and she managed money with the astuteness of a Scottish banker. As a result, she had accumulated a small but solid estate that, combined with her job, promised to keep her comfortable for the rest of her years. For Annie Lou, Napoleon's message was interesting on an intellectual level, and its affect on Leila was something she could deeply appreciate. But gradually she became more and more fascinated with Hill himself. Here was a man of letters and accomplishment, a thinker, an intellectual equal who lived his life as a quiet, respectful gentleman yet could rise before a group of people and whip them into hypnotic flights of intensity and hope. This, thought Annie Lou, might be a man worth getting to know.

Annie Lou was not the type to throw herself at a man, and she did not change her style for Napoleon. Instead, she relied on her innate warmth and charm to win his attention. She was a woman who easily and naturally expanded the normal greetings in the office or at home into conversations simply by asking polite questions. When Napoleon took ill, Annie Lou made sure he had a plentiful supply of hot soup and nourishment—though she also made sure it was Leila, not her, who prepared and delivered the meals. Annie Lou's code of dignity would not allow for forwardness.

By the autumn of 1941, Napoleon and Annie Lou were openly interested in one another. It was not a whirlwind romance—Annie Lou had no interest in short-lived flings and still felt no compulsion to marry until someone could prove to her that it offered something better than she already had. And Napoleon's scars from his mercurial relationship with Rosa Lee were still fresh enough to restrain his impulsiveness. Instead, they began as friends, two people who just enjoyed one another's company. They went out to dinner, took evening walks, and went on country drives. Much of their interaction involved Leila and Charles. The four developed a genuine affection for one another and shared many hours together.

As 1941 wound down, Napoleon Hill's sense of purpose had been rejuvenated, and his sense of self-worth was fully restored. His marriage to Rosa Lee and the personal ruin it had brought were a distant memory, something he could laugh about. For, although he had only modest earnings for the year, 1941 had proved in all other respects to be one of the best years of his life. He had accomplished so much. *Mental Dynamite* was completed, his lectures had won him a great following in the region, and his romance with Annie Lou was in full bloom.

In addition, in William Jacobs he had found an ally who sincerely and completely embraced Hill's philosophy of success, and who used his immense influence in the South and in the federal government to spread the word. The text of an address Jacobs delivered on March 27, 1941, to the U.S. Senate's Southern Policy Committee indicates how artfully Jacobs applied Hill's principles and even his terminology— and to what august minds Jacobs could deliver the message: "[The] topic, 'Going the Extra Mile' is selected for discussion this evening because it presents a thought which is of utmost importance in our present emergency," began Jacobs. His theme was how the South could contribute to the industrial output of war material that was already at a critical stage even though the United States was not yet militarily involved in war in Europe. He spoke of individuals, communities, corporations, and states that were looking for "something for nothing" in the scramble for defense contracts, then proposed a "counter crusade" for "going the extra mile in America."

"[This] ideal is not only altruistic but it is also practical and profitable," Jacobs argued. "It enables one to benefit from the law of increasing returns and the law of compensation."

For nearly an hour, Jacobs lectured, cajoled, and inspired a roomful of powerful senators on the related subjects of war readiness, national values, individual commitment, and the untapped potential contributions of the South. The power of his address stemmed from his ability to blend the language of Hill's philosophy of achievement with his own expert recitation of production statistics and manufacturing trends.

Napoleon would have only one other mentor—W. Clement Stone—who would combine such great personal stature and dedication to the Hill-authored principles of success. No wonder, then, that one of Hill's favorite memories of this period was the role he played in helping Jacobs accomplish a key victory in his personal campaign to lure Northern industrialists to the South.

Hill's contribution was the writing of a truly immodest proposal that Dr. Jacobs presented to the directors of four utility companies in North and South Carolina. The proposal sought to convince the four companies to underwrite a large-scale market survey of Northern industrial firms. The survey was designed both to tout the benefits of locating businesses in the South and to identify the best corporate prospects for relocation based on their answers to the survey questions. The tricky part was the cost. Jacobs and Hill had determined that the project would require a budget of one hundred thousand dollars to have any chance of success—and one hundred thousand dollars was still considered a hefty chunk of money, even for substantial power companies, in 1941.

So Hill massaged the written proposal with a full treatment of his most artful sales prose. And to this convincing document Jacobs added his own pragmatic touch: When the directors asked, "How much?" Jacobs sincerely replied, "Two hundred thousand dollars." The directors responded in a predictable fashion: They expressed shock at the amount, conjured new respect for the project because of its obvious magnitude and potential impact, then countered with a half-off offer. They offered to put up one hundred thousand dollars, and Jacobs accepted immediately.

By the end of 1941, the Jacobs survey was in the mail, the first pressrun of *Mental Dynamite* was in distribution, and Hill and Jacobs were busily lining up textile plants and other places of business for Hill's Philosophy of American Achievement course.

Then, on the dawn of December 7, 1941, fate interceded once again. The unrestrained might unleashed by a Japanese armada of aircraft carriers devastated Pearl Harbor; within twenty-four hours, the United States ended months of fence-sitting and divisive internal debate and formally entered World War II. With the declaration of war on the Axis powers came sudden, sweeping changes in America. Hundreds of thousands of combat-aged young men left the workforce and school campuses to join the armed forces, the nation's industrial might quickly became absolutely dedicated to the production of military materials, and civilian consumption of an ever-growing list of war-essential commodities became severely rationed.

Barely had America entered the war when the federal government added paper to the list of rationed commodities. What little paper was left for nonessential use was oppressively expensive and hard to get. With the first, small pressrun of *Mental Dynamite* nearly sold out and no paper available for a second pressrun, Hill's sixteen-volume text became an early war casualty. Philosophy of American Achievement courses would fall next; it was just a matter of time since students were becoming almost as rare as the textbooks. Jacobs offered to keep Napoleon on his payroll when the two agreed to put their plans on hold for the duration of the war, but Hill couldn't accept what he perceived as charity. And so, with the same suddenness that America found itself at war, Napoleon Hill found himself once again out of work—this time at the age of fifty-seven and located in the rural environs of the Deep South.

Millions of Americans found themselves in similarly shocking, sudden transitions because of the war. Of them all, no one was more prepared to deal with the situation than Napoleon Hill. After a lifetime of conquests and cataclysms, the sudden turn of events brought on by the war was a familiar script for Hill—and not especially unpleasant, either. As one who passionately believed what he preached, he considered life's great calamities a prelude to life's great achievements. When he sat down to ponder his next step with Annie Lou and Leila, whatever regrets he had about the fate of *Mental Dynamite* and his Philosophy of American Achievement classes were overwhelmed by a sense of anticipation about the next adventure. America was suffering one crushing battlefield setback after another in the early days of its participation in the war. Her only hope was to hold on tenaciously at the front lines while the people at home revved up the country's potentially overwhelming military-industrial machine as fast as possible. There was so much to be done that the hardest decision was where to start. What was worth doing? And, was there anything he could do that would keep him close enough to Annie Lou to continue their gentle courtship?

Napoleon Hill's war calling came, fittingly enough, from one of America's most idealistic and creative entrepreneurs. R. G. LeTourneau owned a sprawling, giant manufacturing empire that, along with a handful of other firms, produced most of the heavy construction machinery used in the Allied nations and nearly all the heavy equipment used in America.

The outbreak of World War II brought crushing waves of orders for LeTourneau Company's leviathan scrapers, cranes, rooters, pullers, and rollers. The company's machines were designed for huge construction projects such as roads, airfields, bridges, and dams—the very construction America was undertaking at a feverish pace within her own boundaries and at hundreds of strategic locations throughout the unoccupied world. The company had survived decades of booms and busts, mainly on the strength of R. G. LeTourneau's creative genius. Though he never attended high school, LeTourneau was an extraordinarily gifted tinkerer whose self-taught design and engineering prowess produced more than two hundred patents in his career. Led by his personal flair for innovation, the company had become a wellspring of unique machines that radically improved production rates for major construction projects. Such machines were vital to the Allied war effort.

The avalanche of orders overwhelmed LeTourneau's manufacturing facilities in Illinois, Mississippi, and Georgia. Having struggled for most of a decade to get enough volume to keep the plants open with skeletal workforces, suddenly LeTourneau Company was hiring at a frantic pace, adding shifts, and begging for overtime from its core workers . . . while also scrambling to find reliable sources for the steel, components, and other manufacturing materials it suddenly needed in far greater volume than ever before.

Nowhere was the ensuing chaos more ominous than at LeTourneau's massive plant in Toccoa, Georgia, a Clinton-sized community about one hundred miles west of Clinton. With the tide of new orders had come waves of dissension in the workforce and alarming declines in productivity and quality. Absenteeism among the factory's two thousand employees more than doubled in just a few months. Complaints about working conditions increased exponentially; on one day, thirty such complaints were lodged with management. And with the unrest came labor union organizers armed with an extravagant war chest, intent on seizing the rare opportunity to establish labor unions in the South.

For R. G. LeTourneau and his managers, the situation was terrifying. If they couldn't solve the productivity and quality problems, they faced the very real prospect of failure. Having survived the scarcities of the depression, they were now choking on the bountiful demands of the war.

In addition to business considerations, the union organizers represented a very personal issue for R. G. LeTourneau. Unlike traditional union-bashers of the day, LeTourneau's opposition to trade unions wasn't financial, it was philosophical. He was a deeply religious man with utopian dreams. He would eventually use his personal wealth to build hospitals, schools, and missionary outposts. He considered his manufacturing empire an opportunity to create a social model for capitalism—an organization in which everyone worked for the common good and was rewarded with fair pay, security, and the satisfaction of success.

The problem LeTourneau had with trade unions was that, honest or corrupt, they advocated loyalty to the union and suspicion, if not outright hostility, to the company. So deeply did LeTourneau feel about this issue that, when a union finally did organize one of his factories, he sold the company. But, thanks in part to Napoleon Hill, that event would not take place for nearly two more decades.

The management of LeTourneau's Toccoa plant convened regular roundtable meetings in a continuing search for solutions to their mounting crisis. At one such meeting, the group closely questioned a young manager whose operation showed little evidence of the unrest that infected the rest of the plant.

The manager ascribed his success to Hill's book, *Think and Grow Rich!* He had given it to his foremen to read and frequently discussed with them how they could apply Hill's principles to the problems they faced in the factory. When R. G. LeTourneau was briefed on the meeting, he instructed Toccoa's general manager to recruit Hill to come to the plant as a consultant.

For Napoleon Hill, the LeTourneau offer was an ideal situation. On a personal level, Toccoa was close enough to Clinton to allow weekend courtship of Annie Lou. Gas rationing was no problem because LeTourneau, as a major defense contractor, could get him priority status for coupons. The 109-mile drive between Toccoa and Clinton was pleasant, too—fine U.S. Highways linked the two communities, and traffic was light due to gas rationing.

On a professional level, the LeTourneau situation was the opportunity of a lifetime. While the philosophy of success had been applied many times over the years to business situations, it was usually employed to improve a company's sales function. Finally, Hill would have a chance to put his principles to work in a factory, to show the world that wage-earning men and women would respond to his philosophy just as constructively and quickly as salespeople and managers—and that once labor and management were speaking the same language, any goal that could be conceived could also be achieved.

And, finally, the LeTourneau challenge gave Hill a chance to realize the goals that had brought him to Clinton in the grim aftermath of his divorce. He could strike a significant victory for Southern industrialism by helping Toccoa's management team make their factory the company's model plant. And he could do it with his Philosophy of American Achievement lectures, thus providing a glorious and significant climax to the work he and William Jacobs had undertaken. *Mental Dynamite* might have been a casualty of war, but the gospel of self-improvement and success would become an integral part of the war effort.

It took little time for Hill to unearth the specific sources of LeTourneau Company's problems in Toccoa. They were the same problems that had plagued American companies since the age of industrialization came to the continent in the 1890s. Hill had written about these problems frequently, especially in the pages of *Hill's Golden Rule* and *Napoleon Hill's Magazine*. Both magazines counted a great many laborers among their readers, people who came to Hill to find a way to a better life. As he guided and inspired them, Hill also learned about the life they wished to leave. LeTourneau was a textbook example.

R. G. LeTourneau's idealism and the company's fair-wage policy notwithstanding, there remained a large gulf between Toccoa's managers and the hourly workforce. As at most American plants of the day, LeTourneau's managers did the thinking and gave the orders; the workforce existed simply to do the work. The workers were taken for granted until, with the intense strain of the war-effort orders, they rebelled. There was seemingly nothing in the backbreaking, bleary-eyed work pace for them but drudgery and fatigue and unrelenting pressure to produce more, faster, and better.

Hill tackled the problem systematically. He began by starting Philosophy of American Achievement classes for Toccoa's top management people. The classes covered all seventeen principles of success (the number had increased as Hill refined his philosophy), with each principle discussed on two levels: how it applied to each individual manager, and how it applied to the people they supervised. The beauty of Hill's philosophy was that, though written for the individual, it could easily and logically be applied to groups, too—even companies.

Definiteness of purpose, Hill taught, is the basis for all

achievement. He made his students define their real goals, made them separate minor annoyances and frustrations from the basic objectives of their careers and their responsibilities within LeTourneau. They then talked about hourly workers having a definite purpose—for their personal lives and for their work in the plant, even if the latter was a temporary stop on their road to success.

One by one, the LeTourneau managers came to realize that workers with a definite purpose in life were not a threat to the company. On the contrary, when their definite purpose in the plant could be married to their goals in life, the company would benefit.

Thus did goals and goal setting lead to a discussion of the Master Mind principle. At the LeTourneau plant, this involved getting hourly and salaried employees alike to commit themselves to accomplishing the company's goals. Impossible? Not if everyone has a definite purpose that can be advanced through the accomplishment of company goals, said Hill. Whether the individual's goal is security of employment or career advancement or simply job satisfaction, he or she will benefit from a Master Mind Alliance because the company will succeed and the individual's responsibility, having been clearly defined at the outset, will be clearly recognized when the group succeeds.

Few concepts in factory management were more idealistic in 1942 than Hill's Master Mind principle. But LeTourneau's company culture had its share of idealism, too, and Toccoa's managers received Hill's words with open minds. How, they wondered, could they ever break through the barriers time had wrought between them and the workers to engage in goal setting and create a Master Mind Alliance? One by one, Hill worked through the other fifteen principles, showing how to use each to create harmony and trust in the plant.

The lesson on developing a pleasing personality was one

of the first and most important discussions that followed. "A pleasing personality," said Hill, "is your key to motivating others to help you achieve goals." He then took his students through more than two dozen characteristics of a pleasing personality and challenged each individual to apply each characteristic to his or her own work. First came a positive attitude—nothing could be more demoralizing than working for someone who is angry, frustrated or lacking commitment to the group's goals. Flexibility of mind was equally important, said Hill, because it gives the supervisor the ability to understand and sympathize with someone else.

On he went through sincerity of purpose, decisiveness, courtesy, tactfulness, using a pleasing tone of voice, tolerance, frankness, and displaying a good sense of humor. In its totality, the Pleasing Personality lesson was a course in nurturing human dignity, in recognizing and responding to the needs and desires of others, in creating harmony by creating an environment of mutual respect. It was an extreme departure from the standard management practices of the day, yet as Hill laid out each simple point, his audience saw the logic of the concept.

In lectures and discussion groups, Toccoa's top managers received instruction on the other principles—from personal initiative and going the extra mile to self-discipline, accurate thinking, creativity, and applying the Golden Rule.

Life at the Toccoa plant began to change. The managers were as inspired by Napoleon Hill as any other group in his long, illustrious career, and they completely embraced his reasoned approach to individual and group achievement. They put each lesson to work and saw improvement almost immediately—not a sweeping, miracle cure but subtle, positive changes in their interpersonal relationships with each other and with the supervisors and foremen who reported to them.

Soon, the executives expanded Hill's work to include

classes for floor supervisors, foremen, and leadmen—and got the same results. Previously taciturn employees responded with disbelief, then guarded interest as their supervisors curtailed order-giving in favor of discussions about goals—and made a noticeable effort to be courteous and enthusiastic. Little by little, the employees responded in kind, and LeTourneau's vital Toccoa operation began to move in a new, more promising direction.

To their credit, LeTourneau's management team provided ideal clay from which a reformer like Hill might mold new attitudes between management and labor. Guided by R. G. LeTourneau's utopian dreams, they were neither antagonistic to labor nor threatened by Hill's iconoclastic solutions. Indeed, they were so enthusiastic about the potential for Hill's tenets that they asked him to bring the course to the workers themselves and, later, to the entire town of Toccoa.

By the end of 1942, when the company decided to expand the Hill program to the entire plant, Toccoa was well on its way to achieving a once unthinkable transformation. In October, plant superintendent Joe Salvador observed that there were noticeable improvements in the plant. He was particularly impressed with the career-expanding changes that had come over some of his lieutenants. "There were several men here who are taking this course whose advancement was limited due to their personalities," he wrote. "Although the course is not completed, a noticeable improvement can be seen in these men . . . chiefly, that they are getting along nicely with men with whom they formerly clashed."

Six weeks later, Salvador's production manager, Earl Rhoads, wrote to Dr. William Jacobs to thank him for his role in creating the Philosophy of American Achievement. "It is not possible to estimate its value to those of us who were associated in this class," wrote Rhoads. "It has already been of very definite value to me and the same declaration has been made by many others in this group. The lessons on a Definite

Major Purpose, Personality, Mental Attitude, and Applied Faith have produced results of inestimable value."

The company's enthusiasm for the Philosophy of American Achievement course was well placed. By the end of 1943, employee complaints had trickled down to an average of one a week, absenteeism had dwindled to an amazing three percent, productivity was at a four-year high, and the workforce had rejected the union organizers. On December 27, 1943, Jack Salvador, the vice president and general manager of LeTourneau Company of Georgia, and three of his executives composed a letter of gratitude to Hill, acknowledging the great changes he had inspired in less than two years. "An enduring satisfaction you will have from the friendship the employees and officials here hold for you," they wrote, "is that our friendship will be held fast by the permanent benefits you have interwoven into your friendship with us."

In the years to come, Napoleon Hill would cite LeTourneau frequently as an example of learning from adversity and the power of the Master Mind principle and teamwork. From the brink of disaster in the early days of 1942, LeTourneau recovered to enjoy overwhelming success for the rest of the decade and to win stature and praise for its valuable contributions to the war effort. It was one of the most impressive applications of Hill's principles of success. Ironically, many of the same theories would be put to work on a grand scale in postwar Japanese factories and would find their way back to American industry four decades later.

While Napoleon spent weekdays on the Toccoa reformation, he spent most of his weekends in Clinton, where his courtship of Annie Lou proceeded at a serene pace. Annie Lou would not be hurried, and for once in his life, Napoleon himself sampled the sweetness of life taken at a languorous gait.

Perhaps if Annie Lou had settled for anything less, their

unlikely romance would never have developed. They were a study in opposites, a crowd-pleasing man with a flair for flash counterbalanced by a private woman given to moderation and understatement. He created, she conserved. He made and lost fortunes, she managed resources. He criticized, she forgave. He was spontaneous, she deliberate. A friend once joked that theirs was a platonic relationship—"play" for Napoleon, "tonic" for Annie Lou. In fact, however, it was tonic for Napoleon, whose lifetime of relationships with women— even Florence—had been as unsettled as his career.

First they became friends, then close friends, then intimates. It was Annie Lou's way. Nor was theirs a relationship between just two people. Annie Lou was part of a family and a lifelong network of friends, and during the two years of their courtship, Napoleon was drawn into Annie Lou's circle and began to share her roots, especially her attachment with Leila and her son Charles.

As Napoleon's work in Toccoa began winding down in 1943, Napoleon and Annie Lou decided to get married. The ceremony was as simple and elegant as their courtship had been. Their marriage took place the day before Christmas in the apartment shared by Annie Lou and Leila. Because of Napoleon's divorces, the local Baptist minister would not conduct the ceremony. Therefore, they were married by Dr. Dudley Jones, the former pastor of Clinton's First Presbyterian Church; he was assisted by none other than Dr. William Jacobs.

Annie Lou's niece played the wedding music, and Leila sang "The Sweetest Story Ever Told." Annie Lou and Napoleon exchanged vows before a beautiful antique fireplace mantel bedecked in Christmas flowers and greenery.

Even so practiced a player as Napoleon Hill had to marvel at the inconceivable changes that time could create. Just two years earlier, he had endured a Christmas of isolation, financial ruin, and personal humiliation. Now he had a strong, loving wife, an extended family, and in both Clinton and Toccoa some of the finest friends he would ever know.

Annie Lou and Napoleon left on their honeymoon in the midst of joy and sadness: joy because they had found each other and had built the foundation for a long, loving marriage; sadness because life's great adventure beckoned them away. Their honeymoon would take them to Toccoa for celebration and farewells with Napoleon's close friends and associates at LeTourneau, then to California, where they would sample a new life together.

It may have been nothing more than wanderlust that pulled Napoleon away from Clinton in the winter of 1943, but Annie Lou exercised her charm and foresight to make sure he had a plan. He did, and it was a good one. At fifty-nine years of age, Napoleon wanted to plow new ground with his business evangelism. California was the perfect place, with its booming wartime economy, rapid population growth, and gentle climate. Although he had made few appearances in California, he was a well-known author in the state and could expect large audiences for his lectures. His preliminary research had revealed that *Think and Grow Rich!* was so popular in Los Angeles that the public library there still kept more than seventy copies of the book on its shelves. Napoleon told Annie Lou he could fill lecture halls for years to come in such a place, and he was right.

For the rest of the decade, Hill lived a delicious life. He delivered his Philosophy of American Achievement lectures frequently, but seldom far from home. He received an honorary doctor of literature degree from Pacific International University, which thereupon appointed him to head the school's new Department of Industrial Philosophy. The intent was to teach the LeTourneau story to California industrialists; Hill's activities in that pursuit served to extend his popularity as a speaker, though his affect on industrial relations in California was far more modest than it had been at LeTourneau.

Between his university activities and his own lecturing and consulting enterprise, Hill earned a comfortable income, and he and Annie Lou had plenty of time to enjoy life together. By 1947, however, at the age of sixty-three, Hill started showing signs of restlessness. He commanded a huge following and still drew large, enthusiastic crowds wherever he spoke. But he needed a new challenge to shake off the monotony of success. To satisfy this urge, he negotiated an agreement with KFWB Radio, a major independent station broadcasting from Hollywood, to broadcast a thirty-minute program from 3:30 to 4:00 P.M. every Sunday. Although he butted heads with very popular network programs in this time slot, his show was a great success. Over the next several years, hundreds of thousands of Californians had the opportunity to hear Hill expound on his philosophy of success. Part of his compensation was advertising time for his lectures, books, and consulting services, and, according to KFWB management, Hill's program pulled more direct-response mail than any of the station's other Sunday afternoon programming.

The success of Napoleon's radio show led to ever more requests for his oratory, especially by companies and business groups. For the three-year duration of the show, Hill traveled, wrote, and lectured at the breakneck pace he had endured as a young man. In his early sixties, he had the physical appearance of a forty-five-year-old, the charm of a thirty-five-year-old, and the energy of a teenager.

While Napoleon pursued his lifelong crusade for personal achievement, Annie Lou managed his business and the household. Pragmatic and iron-willed about things that counted, Annie Lou helped Napoleon stay focused on his goals and curtail his tendency to pursue too many projects at once. She also steered him around the con men and charlatans who had always found in the guileless Hill an easy mark.

But more than business, Annie Lou gave Napoleon the only real family life he ever knew in his adult years. She gave him emotional and spiritual support, maintained their friendships with the people back home in Clinton and Toccoa with a steady stream of warm letters and thoughtful cards, and accompanied Hill on many of his trips. She also wrote frequently to Napoleon's sons, David, Blair, and James. They accepted her as a warm and sincere person and, through her advocacy, David and Blair resumed the practice of corresponding through holiday and birthday notes with Napoleon. His sons' notes were more cordial than warm—Annie Lou's attempts to foster a full reconciliation between sons and father never met with full success—but they helped Napoleon overcome the guilt and regret he harbored about his earlier failings. In that sense, Napoleon's life—and perhaps his sons' lives as well—was richer for Annie Lou's efforts.

As Napoleon neared his sixty-fifth birthday in 1949, he made a conscious decision to reduce his workload. He wasn't ready for retirement yet, but he wanted more time with Annie Lou, more time to savor the free and easy California lifestyle, and more time to review, reflect, and contemplate what was going on around him. It had been a half century since he left Wise County for the first time in search of fame and fortune. And although he had found both, it had been a fast and wild ride. He had earned a retirement but knew he couldn't live that way, so he settled for a "semiretirement." He resigned from his radio job, continued his writing as a hobby, and took a limited number of public speaking engagements. It was just the right mix of leisure and work. Annie Lou loved it and so did Napoleon. Indeed, as 1950 came and went, Napoleon noted with a chuckle that he had finally completed ten consecutive years in his life without a personal catastrophe. He had finally experienced ease and contentment in life, and he couldn't think of any reason to change it.

Indeed, on May 2, 1951, Hill and Annie Lou drew up a one-page statement of their "immediate major purposes." The signed document focused on income strategies for Nap's semiretirement years. One point called for income from sales of Hill's *Law of Success* home-study textbooks, two others dealt with the marketing of *Believe and You Shall Achieve,* a manuscript Hill was working on at the time. Another item dealt with collection of a debt from an associate in Rio de Janeiro, and yet another focused on finding sponsors for a television program based on the seventeen principles of success. Few people would associate such an ambitious set of short-term goals with retirement, but Napoleon did. The sixth and final item in the document read, "A sufficient income from all the above sources to take care of all our NEEDS and PERSONAL DESIRES, for the remainder of our lives, without further major efforts on our part, we having already earned the right to this income by past services rendered."

But even as Napoleon settled back to enjoy his twilight years, fate was spinning yet another web for him. Weeks after drafting and signing his retirement statement, he would fulfill an earlier agreement to speak before a dental convention in Chicago . . . and by fulfilling this obligation, his life and the lives of countless others would be forever changed.

Shortly before Hill's engagement in Chicago, Dr. Herb Gustafson, a Chicago-based dentist who had recommended Hill as a speaker, picked up the phone to repay a favor to one of his favorite patients and finest friends.

The man he was calling had introduced him to Napoleon Hill's work some years earlier by giving him a copy of *Think and Grow Rich!* The two men had often discussed success, especially the human qualities that success required and formulas that people could follow to accomplish great things in their lives. Dr. Gustafson's friend was something of a philosopher himself and had seized on *Think and Grow Rich!* as a great work when it first came out. In fact, Dr. Gustafson's friend had personally purchased several thousand copies of the book over the years, distributing them to his employees and friends.

Gustafson's call was quickly put through and the high-voltage voice of W. Clement Stone came on the line with a friendly greeting.

"Clem," said Gustafson, "how would you like to hear Napoleon Hill speak next week?"

Stone chuckled. Since Hill had dropped out of the national spotlight some years before, Stone assumed the author-philosopher had died.

"Herb," he replied, "I don't think my time has come yet."

The two friends laughed, then Gustafson delivered his news. Not only was Hill still living, he would be appearing in Chicago the following week at a luncheon where Stone was also speaking. At last he could meet the man who had sold him so many books.

Stone himself had achieved fame as a self-made entrepreneur who had amassed a personal fortune and created a dynamic, far-flung company from selling one-dollar travel-insurance policies. When word reached Napoleon that Stone would attend the luncheon, the sixty-seven-year-old semiretired business evangelist felt a surge of adrenaline. This, Hill thought, could be very interesting.

That sentiment turned out to be one of the rare understatements in Napoleon Hill's long and full life.

CHAPTER 8

1951-1962

Napoleon Hill's adrenaline was still pumping full force when the meeting broke for lunch following his speech.

He had been a smashing success. His highly educated, well-to-do audience had been as captivated and energized by his evangelistic blend of motivational and philosophical messages as any other group he had addressed over the previous fifty years. And while he had enthralled thousands of audiences in his lifetime, the thrill of the experience never eroded. If anything, at age sixty-seven, with his career in the half-speed of semiretirement, the satisfaction from a spine-tingling performance was even greater.

As the cluster of well-wishers and admirers gradually receded and the conventioneers began taking their seats for lunch, W. Clement Stone made his entrance.

Stone was not yet the sort of public figure whose appearance in a crowded room would stop conversations and turn heads. Although he had blazed a wide swath of recognition and respect in the insurance industry, he had no use for publicity and press coverage. He was dedicated to building his business, not a public image, so he tried to stay out of the public limelight. Still, he was a distinctive presence, even to those who didn't know him. Smartly dressed in his trademark dark suit, starched white shirt, and traditional bow tie, Stone radiated energy and self-assurance as he began working the crowd. Not even a Chicago politician was his equal when it came to pressing the flesh with a room full of strangers. He was, after all, the millionaire master of cold-call selling—a man who had amassed a personal fortune selling one-dollar insurance policies without an appointment to people he'd never met before in his life. Nor was he daunted by anyone's station in life: His classic sales strategy was to target a large business—banks were best—and start with the president or the chairman, if the latter were on the premises. After selling the top executive, Stone would work his way down the pecking order to the clerks and maintenance people, pointing out to each prospect that the prospect's boss and the president of the prospect's organization had purchased the same policy.

That strategy, combined with Stone's carefully honed formula for handling the sales situation, had made him an immensely successful salesman; his ability to train others to employ the same strategy and sales tactics had led to the creation of his own army of super salespeople—and a personal fortune for Stone.

Stone's interest in *Think and Grow Rich!* and in Hill himself stemmed directly from his belief that there were formulas one could follow to achieve success—in sales, in a career, and in life. The canvassing strategies he employed were one kind of formula, the "scripts" he created for his salespeople and himself to use in the selling situation were another kind of formula. But Stone knew that a truly successful salesperson needed more than a script and a basic strategy. He or she also needed a philosophical formula that would help them shake off the despair of a bad day or week, overcome the contentedness that could follow a great week, and resolve the inevitable conflicts between career and family, ambition and principles, and the many other doubts and dichotomies that can erode one's performance.

Hill's principles of success were a near perfect adjunct to Stone's own selling formulas and disciplines. Indeed, from the time he read *Think and Grow Rich!* in 1938, there were two absolutes in Stone's business: Every new salesperson he hired was trained in Stone's formula—many by Stone himself— and each of the thousands of salespeople in his organization got a copy of *Think and Grow Rich!* from Stone . . . and was required to read it.

True to his word, Herb Gustafson ushered Stone to the speaker's table and sat him next to Hill. As Gustafson completed the introductions, Stone enthusiastically told Hill that he was one of Hill's biggest customers, having purchased thousands of copies of *Think and Grow Rich!* for his salespeople over the past decade. He also told Hill that the book had been instrumental in his rise to great wealth.

Napoleon beamed with delight. Praise was something he always valued from any source. Praise from accomplished men and women was even more stimulating. But this was more than praise. It was an endorsement of his life's work, and it came from a man who was more than accomplished— Stone was, in Hill's eyes, an empire builder cut from the same mold as the giants of early twentieth-century American industry whose philosophies had provided the basis for Hill's principles of success.

Hill's quiet semiretirement fell into jeopardy as Stone finished his brief greeting. After nearly a half century of trials and tribulations, Hill's mission from Carnegie had come full circle. He had assembled, analyzed, and popularized the qualities that bred the greatest figures in American business history, and had lived to meet a man whose modern greatness was linked through Hill's own work to those of Carnegie's generation. Suddenly, Hill was only aware of how much more could be done.

W. Clement Stone was on the same wavelength. A life-long goal setter, by 1952, he had two primary goals. His business goal was to build his thirty-million-dollar empire to the one-hundred-million-dollar level. His personal goal was to use his wealth and knowledge to "create a better world for this and future generations." Stone would later refer to this altruistic resolve as his "magnificent obsession," after reading Lloyd C. Douglas's *The Magnificent Obsession.* The connection between Stone's goals and Hill's rejuvenated sense of activism became clear to both men as the luncheon progressed.

"If you want to know someone," Stone taught his sales-people, "get them to talk about themselves." Stone applied his own teachings to his first meeting with Hill. He broke the ice by asking questions about Hill's speech. He quickly found it didn't take much to get Napoleon Hill started. Even at age sixty-seven, Hill spoke with an unrelenting intensity and animation that kept even a veteran listener like Stone on the edge of his seat. Soon, Stone's questions were no longer inspired by polite curiosity. He began probing the depths of a man whose energy, ideas, and captivating delivery could have a tremendous impact on his business and his humanitarian goals.

By the end of the luncheon, Hill and Stone had carved the foundation for a Master Mind Alliance. They had debated Hill's belief that the most important principle of success was a definite major purpose—Stone believed a positive mental attitude came first—and they had shared anecdotes and philosophies on a wide range of subjects. As the creative sparks flew, Stone turned on his most persuasive selling charm and told Hill he should forget about retirement and come back to a world that needed him as much as it ever had.

Hill countered with the wisdom gained from a half century of accomplishment and failure: He would do just that—

provided Stone himself would manage his activities. Napoleon had learned all too well that there was more to spreading a great message than a great delivery; to be really successful, one needed organization, pragmatic planning, and powerful backing. W. Clement Stone could offer all these qualities and more—and he did.

In the speeches and writings of his lifetime, Napoleon Hill offered dozens, perhaps hundreds of different examples of Master Mind Alliances, but none would ever achieve the scope, depth, longevity, and impact of the alliance that he and Stone forged over the ensuing months and decades. They would never have a contract; their working agreement would always be based on common goals, and their business relationship was based on trust and a handshake.

In August 1952, after Napoleon completed the remainder of his public-appearance obligations, Stone put Hill on his payroll and their partnership began in earnest with the formation of Napoleon Hill Associates. Still living in California, Napoleon plunged into the creation of a new book as well as the new home-study textbooks that he and Stone had decided were central to their project. He also commuted regularly to Chicago to help Stone design and implement a new training program for Stone's salespeople.

While Hill's contributions to the training program for Combined Insurance Company of America were perhaps overshadowed in his own mind by the books he created during the same period, Stone was fully aware of his new associate's prodigious efforts—and the prodigious results that developed. Stone's previous approach to sales training focused on new employees: He or one of his sales managers would take new salespeople out on calls, show them how to apply the strategy and scripts, then stay with the initiate long enough to ensure that he or she had mastered the process. Following that introduction, salesmanship was reinforced

mainly through Stone's daily sales letters, which were a mixture of motivational messages and reviews of basic selling
principles.

Despite the legendary success of his sales force, Stone
believed that the performance of even his best salespeople
could be dramatically improved if they received periodic
face-to-face retraining and reinforcement. He also believed
that this was the key to Combined's continued growth.

Stone's new training program called for assembling
groups of salespeople for several days at a time to review the
company's basic sales strategies and tactics, to drill them on
new and old formulas for handling a wide variety of sales situations, and, most of all, to rejuvenate their enthusiasm.

The availability of Napoleon Hill to work in this program was a rich blessing, and Stone knew it. Not only could
Hill brew great froths of inspiration anywhere people gathered, but his message—his philosophy—would stay with
them even after the echoes of his spoken words faded to
silence and their world became once again a place where
failure lurked along the trail to each day's opportunities.

Many of Stone's salespeople had outspoken doubts about
this new program, despite the boss's enthusiastic promotion
of it. They were concerned about losing time in the field,
they questioned the need for scripts and role-playing, and,
most of all, they could conceive no earthly benefit from a discourse on the philosophy of success by a man whose book on
the subject they had already read.

But that came before they experienced the program.
Afterward, it was a different story. Literally hundreds of
Combined salespeople found themselves operating at new
performance levels as they applied both the latest "blue-
prints" for selling created by Stone and Hill's time-tested
principles of success for meeting the challenges of life and
career.

Despite his gift for hyperbole in describing his own accomplishments, not even Napoleon Hill could embellish on his actual contribution to the remarkable ensuing growth of Stone's empire. Through the rest of the fifties, Combined Insurance Company's sales increased at a dizzying pace, and Stone used the profits to expand into disability and life insurance by acquiring more companies, which themselves enjoyed tremendous growth. Ultimately, Stone's thirty-million-dollar company would reach nearly nine-hundred-million dollars in assets, and Stone himself would trace much of the company's success to the man he lured out of retirement in 1952.

"I really hit the jackpot with Napoleon Hill," Stone remarked many years later. "Motivation was the key to growing from where we were in 1952, and nobody could motivate people like Napoleon Hill."

But the profitability and growth of Combined Insurance Company of America was only a by-product of the Stone-Hill Master Mind Alliance. Their definite main purpose was to improve their own society—and later, others—by communicating the principles of success to millions of people of all walks of life, of all races and religions. The organization they established to accomplish all this was based on altruistic goals, but it was not a charity. Napoleon Hill Associates would produce books, courses, lectures, inspirational films, radio programs, and, later, television shows. These activities would generate revenues to perpetuate the organization's work. Both Hill and Stone would often donate their time and cover their own expenses to take their message to the poor, but their philanthropic enterprise was set up like a business. It would generate profits to cover employee salaries—including Hill's—and to create capital for new programs and products.

In 1953, the first products of the Stone-Hill Master Mind Alliance began to appear. In May, the first of six *Science of Success* textbooks was published. Later renamed *PMA Science of Success,* the six volumes comprised a home-study course in the seventeen laws of success—Stone's concept of a positive mental attitude had been added to Hill's original principles. They used the textbooks for classes and lectures sponsored and promoted by Napoleon Hill Associates, and they secured accreditation for the home-study course from the National Home Study Council in Washington, D.C. Through the rest of the decade, public acceptance of and participation in both formats grew rapidly.

In June of 1953, the partners published a book by Hill entitled *How to Raise Your Own Salary.* It was one of two obscure books Hill had written during his semiretirement; in the earliest days of Napoleon Hill Associates, Stone and Hill had purchased both works from the California publisher who had originally printed them. One, *The Master Key to Riches,* would not be reissued until 1965. The other, originally published as *Think Your Way to Wealth,* was revised and released as *How to Raise Your Own Salary.*

The 1953 release was calculated to renew public awareness of and interest in Hill's philosophy. It covered the principles of success via a somewhat contrived conversational format featuring Hill and Andrew Carnegie. While *How to Raise Your Own Salary* was not one of Hill's finest works, it served to demonstrate the huge impact W. Clement Stone's management and marketing expertise could have in getting Hill's thoughts communicated to the masses. Backed by a monumental, multimedia promotional effort that far exceeded the combined promotions for all of Hill's previous works, the book became an immediate best-seller. It was advertised on radio and television, in newspapers and magazines, and through point-of-purchase displays in bookstores. In addition, the partners saturated the nation's media with review copies, then arranged for Hill to be interviewed by dozens of radio, television, and newspaper journalists.

Sales were boosted by many, many glowing reviews, none

more influential than that of radio and television broadcaster Earl Nightingale. Nightingale, who plied his trade for WGN, a giant Chicago radio and television broadcasting company, enjoyed a personal friendship with W. Clement Stone and had admired Hill since reading *Think and Grow Rich!* more than a decade earlier.

"Napoleon Hill's work changed my life," Nightingale told Stone in a letter. "In more than 20 years spent searching for a formula with which a person could utilize every possible element in his favor, it was not until I read Napoleon Hill that I found the answers. . . . On studying *Think and Grow Rich!* I realized I had already known Napoleon Hill's principles. But he expressed them in a nutshell—a guide that would help me achieve any worthwhile goal."

Given an opportunity to express his admiration and gratitude to Hill, Nightingale took it upon himself to promote *How to Raise Your Own Salary* on WGN radio for a week, without charge. Afterward, Stone and Hill hired Nightingale to an endorsement contract—and found that his radio endorsements sold more copies of the book than all their other promotional efforts combined.

Weeks after the debut of Hill's revised book, Stone and Hill embarked on one of the most unique endeavors in modern self-help journalism. The project was the filming of a documentary-style testimonial to the potent changes that result when the principles of success are applied by groups of people. *A New Sound In Paris* covered the story of how an eight-week course taught by Napoleon Hill in 1952 changed the fortunes of the entire town of Paris, Missouri. The film would ultimately be seen by hundreds of thousands of people and was considered by Hill, Stone, and the inner circle of Napoleon Hill Associates to be a milestone achievement in the success of the organization.

Like thousands of small towns in postwar America, Paris,

Missouri, was in a gradual social and economic decline in 1952. Located in rural northeastern Missouri, hundreds of miles from any major metropolitan area, the town's fourteen hundred citizens were losing many of their young men and women to the lure of big-city opportunities. Similarly, business commerce in Paris was declining as area farmers, the backbone of the town's trade for decades, were, like millions of other Americans, experiencing the freedoms of mobility— good roads, good cars and trucks, and cheap and plentiful fuel meant they could travel great distances to do their buying. Dollars once spent exclusively in Paris were being siphoned off to larger towns and small cities like Moberly, Mexico, and even Hannibal.

As business declined, investment capital became harder to get. The town's physical appearance began to erode, and so did the morale of the citizens.

Then, in January 1952, a Paris businessman named W. C. "Bill" Robinson arranged for Napoleon Hill to come to Paris to conduct an eight-week course in his philosophy of success for ninety-seven residents. Together, they paid Hill ten thousand dollars for the course.

Robinson was a dynamic and persuasive civic leader who had been a Hill devotee since reading *Think and Grow Rich!* His endorsement was influential enough to get ninety-six other Parisians to sign up for the course.

Not all the townspeople were enthusiastic about the venture. One man in particular suspected that Hill was a fraud and that his course was a latter-day medicine show. This skeptic conducted a wide-reaching background check on Hill and reportedly included inquiries to the FBI, Dun and Bradstreet, and the Better Business Bureau—even though Robinson himself had corresponded with people at LeTourneau Company of Georgia, Dr. William Plumer Jacobs, and many others before arranging for Hill to come to Paris.

Such determined and—to Hill, at least—malevolent detractors were not new to Napoleon. Earlier in life he had conducted long-running professional feuds with such people—and lost two magazines and several other businesses as a result. At age sixty-eight, Hill conceived a whole new approach to damage-seeking critics. In an interview with Mary Granius of *Success Unlimited* magazine a few years later, he described his reaction to his opponent in Paris:

"When I discovered what he was up to . . . I turned the tables on that old saint . . . the only way I ever turned them on anyone who seeks to injure me—by returning good for evil.

"I took every cent of that tuition money and invested it in radio time and gave the course to all the people of the town, plus the people of several surrounding towns and the immediate five counties."

Hill's diplomacy won him acceptance in the community and gave him a unique audience for his teachings. Bill Robinson perpetuated Hill's work by forming a local discussion group known as Club Success Unlimited. Soon modest but visible changes began to occur in Paris. Within a few years, the town boasted ten new storefronts, a new medical clinic, and a resurgence in business activity. Paris would never become a boom town—that was never an objective nor was it a realistic possibility due to the town's location. But it became a solid, economically viable center where people pursued their daily lives with enthusiasm and ambition, and where those who wanted a high quality of life could achieve it.

And that was the message conveyed by *A New Sound in Paris*. The camera showed real people using their own words to describe how their town and their businesses employed their own initiatives to compete happily and successfully in a changing world. The film's power in persuading others to participate wholeheartedly in learning and applying the prin-

ciples of success came from the enthusiasm and personal
anecdotes of the Paris citizens.

Napoleon Hill was sixty-nine years old when he celebrated
the shooting of *A New Sound in Paris* in a letter to Annie Lou.
Composed just after the Thanksgiving of 1953, the letter also
outlined his travel agenda, which was, if anything, even more
demanding than his barnstorming circuits during the *Hill's
Golden Rule* and *Napoleon Hill's Magazine* days.

He would begin the month of December in Chicago, he
told Annie Lou, then he and Stone would set out on a series
of lectures and promotional appearances, to Boston on the
fourteenth, then to New York the same week, then to
Clinton, Iowa, on the twentieth. They would spend
Christmas week in that small river city, then a week in
Miami, and return to Chicago on New Year's Eve. He hoped
to spend the first week of the new year with Annie Lou in
California.

While Hill's schedule was reminiscent of his early days,
several other aspects of his letter were not. Early in his career
his letters were devoted to vague dreams, and to reassuring his
anxious wife—and himself—that great things were just about
to happen. In 1953, under the aegis of W. Clement Stone,
corresponding with a secure and self-sufficient wife, Hill's
thoughts were those of a confident, accomplished man who
had at last found the trail to his life's ambition and who knew
nothing could stop his progress now:

> Business is booming on all fronts. Mr. Stone has quite
> an advertising schedule ordered to begin in January, cov-
> ering among other media, all the life insurance underwrit-
> ers publications. He is still determined to sell a minimum
> of 1,000,000 copies of our book next year and nothing
> can stop him from doing it. . . . A million copies of the
> book will bring us quite a tidy little sum, enough to build

us a new home to our own order and a couple more for
our two sisters, these being the first thing on our agenda
AFTER we get . . . royalties sufficient to pay cash . . . *no
mortgages please.*

Napoleon had often written of great royalties and grand
homes before, but this was no idle dream. Stone's arrangement with Hill assured him of more income than he had ever
earned before. He received a substantial guaranteed salary as
well as a variety of incentives, ranging from royalties on book
sales to commissions on income from lectures and classes. In
addition, during their decade-long partnership, Stone succeeded in purchasing the copyrights to Hill's earlier works,
including *Law of Success* and *Think and Grow Rich!*, and signed
them all over to Hill. In Stone's mind, the copyrights were
not a gift, even though he would not accept Hill's money.
Stone simply believed that authors should retain the rights to
their work—and he had the money to act on his belief.

Ultimately, Stone's greatest contribution to Hill's personal prosperity resulted from Stone's salesmanship. From the
very beginning of their partnership, Stone offered Hill stock
options in Combined Insurance Companies of America—
and convinced his friend that buying into CICA was the
ticket to greater wealth than he had ever known. Hill took
Stone's advice, and by the end of the decade his CICA
stocks alone gave him a net worth of more than one million
dollars.

Stone, quite simply, wanted Hill to be wealthy—it would
not diminish Hill's work ethic, it would take no money from
Stone's own pockets since Stone never wanted financial profits from his magnificent obsession anyway, and Stone felt
most of all that, having spent a lifetime helping others
become rich, Hill deserved his own pot of gold.

And Stone injected one other ingredient into their partnership: He made sure the marriage between Napoleon and

Annie Lou was not overwhelmed by the partners' breakneck business pace. Hill's generous expense account allowed Annie Lou to frequently accompany him to Chicago for business meetings, and Stone often encouraged Napoleon to invite Annie Lou to join him when business took him to popular travel destinations.

On one occasion, Stone proposed that the company pay for Annie Lou to rendezvous with Napoleon in Miami. When Hill objected that he was being too generous, Stone responded, "Annie Lou deserves a better break than to be left alone with all the home responsibilities for a whole year. And after all, you only have one Annie Lou."

Napoleon, of course, was well aware of how precious Annie Lou was to him, and how much they missed one another during his travels. Stone's remark served notice that the boss knew too—and supported their marriage as completely as he supported Hill's work.

Annie Lou's dedication to and support of Napoleon continued unabated. During the fifties, she often traveled with Hill and Stone, contributing her own clear thinking and organizational prowess to the challenges they faced. More important, perhaps, she never let Napoleon lose sight of the most important things in life—friends and family. She sustained their correspondence with dozens of friends around the country, made Nap take time from his peripatetic work schedule to visit relatives, and never stopped trying to reconcile Napoleon and his sons. During the first years of their marriage, she had succeeded in getting Napoleon and his sons to exchange holiday cards and occasional letters; in the decade of the fifties, they would finally reach the point where Nap would come visiting. The visits were short and the longstanding barriers between father and sons were never completely broken down, but the hatred and many of the hurts of decades of estrangement were overcome.

★ ★ ★

Ironically, Napoleon Hill never worked harder or traveled more than he did during the period Annie Lou orchestrated his partial reconciliation with David, James, and Blair. Through the fifties, both Stone and Hill sustained an unrelenting pace to accomplish two primary goals: to spread the philosophy of success to as many people as possible, and to establish solid, profit-making programs that would provide the steady flow of capital Napoleon Hill Associates needed to become a self-sufficient, self-perpetuating organization whose work would continue even after Hill and Stone were gone.

Thanks to Stone's resources and the sheer commitment of both leaders and their associates, they succeeded in spreading the philosophy on a grand scale from the beginning. However, establishing profitable ventures proved much more difficult.

Their advertising support of *How to Raise Your Own Salary* had moved hundreds of thousands of books, but their revenues from book sales did not cover the cost of the advertising. Their early Science of Success classes drew large, enthusiastic audiences and generated pleasing profit margins, but the total revenues generated fell far short of the amounts needed to sustain the organization. To increase revenues, Hill tried to train a cadre of Science of Success instructors so that classes could be run simultaneously all over the country. Unfortunately, the first "Master" course was besieged by personality conflicts and degenerated into a series of complaints and requests for course refunds.

Similarly, efforts by Hill and Stone to market the course to large corporations met with little success. Many targeted companies, including Tupperware, were pleased to have either or both leaders speak at their annual conventions or sales meetings, but none of the firms would commit to full-blown courses.

Napoleon Hill Associates also tried airing fifteen-minute

television lectures, radio shows, and a syndicated newspaper column. In each case, the efforts helped to expand public awareness of Stone and Hill and interest in the Science of Success concept, but none proved to be a profit-making venture.

Like two veteran gladiators of capitalism, however, Stone and Hill were undaunted by the early setbacks. Indeed, they found the challenge invigorating. Calmly, deliberately, they kept searching for the right marketing strategies even as they crisscrossed America spreading their message. And, of course, they ultimately found the strategies and products that worked.

Part of the puzzle came into place in 1954, when Stone and Hill decided to publish a small magazine, *Success Unlimited*. It was a digest-sized, sixteen-page publication carrying the inspirational messages of Stone and Hill to Science of Success students, members of Bill Robinson's Club Success Unlimited, and thousands of others who had been exposed to the philosophy of success through Hill's books and speeches. The magazine was a natural evolution of Hill's early magazine work and Stone's daily inspirational letters to the sales force of Combined Insurance Company of America. And in fact every member of Stone's sales force received a subscription to the new magazine.

Success Unlimited was not itself a profit-making venture at its inception, but it had strategic implications for the organization's future. It was conceived not to expose the uninitiated to the philosophy, but to continue serving those who had heard the message and were trying to apply it to their lives. In the years that followed, the organization would find its financial lifeblood in serving the further needs and interests of the students of the philosophy. Books, recordings, videotapes, and special events would all be offered to burgeoning thousands of graduates and devotees in order to, as Stone put it, "keep the flames of their enthusiasm for self-development alive."

The other important strategy was the decision in 1956 to focus the organization's marketing resources on the home-study course. Stone and Hill changed the name of the course and the textbooks to *PMA Science of Success* and began selling it through direct-mail solicitations. The addition of "PMA" to the title was decisive: through his work for Napoleon Hill Associates, Stone had become a widely heralded public figure and had popularized the concept of a positive mental attitude throughout the country. The linking of Stone's "PMA" and Hill's "Science of Success" redoubled public interest in the course. At the same time, the organization began acquiring expertise in successful direct-mail selling, and its continuity was soon assured.

During those formative years, many public luminaries involved in inspiration and achievement supported the struggling organization. Two whose own fame would continue for decades to come were Earl Nightingale and evangelist Oral Roberts. Still other famous motivators, like Dale Carnegie *(How to Win Friends and Influence People)* and Norman Vincent Peale *(The Power of Positive Thinking),* would participate in the organization's activities as featured speakers in the years to come.

Most of the time and energy that went into creating Napoleon Hill Associates's revenue-generating activities came from the organization's dedicated and loyal staff. Hill and Stone spent most of their time speaking, teaching, writing and, when time allowed, giving interviews to newspaper, radio, and television reporters. Much of this work was in the public interest, producing no revenue at all. The warmest memories of that time for both men came from these appearances.

One such undertaking occurred at an institution called School of the Ozarks in Point Lookout, Missouri. The school provided primary and secondary education for poor children who earned their education by working around the school. The basic tenets of the PMA Science of Success course fit the direction and philosophy of the unique school perfectly, and R. M. Good, the president emeritus of the institution, inquired about adopting the course into their curriculum. Stone and Hill responded enthusiastically—so much so that some members of the school's faculty feared they were dealing with opportunists.

Soon, however, the faculty was convinced of the inherent purity of Hill's and Stone's motives, and of the potential benefits of the course for their students. Ultimately, Hill and Stone both traveled to the school and instructed the teachers in the course, first teaching them the principles, then showing them how to teach the concepts to others. It was a heartwarming success. First the teachers, then the students became infected with enthusiasm, and the course became a fixture in the school's curriculum. Later, R. M. Good reflected on the experiment, saying, "In my opinion, the course was an outstanding success in every way. . . . The effects of [the] course will be of inestimable value to these boys and girls throughout their entire lives. As we look back over this experience and see the accomplishment, we cannot conceive how the course could have worked out more successfully."

But the students and faculty of the school weren't the only ones touched by the event. Stone and Hill fell in love with the school. They wholeheartedly embraced the goals and concepts of School of the Ozarks and quickly developed a lasting affection for the institution's students. They became financial supporters of the school and encouraged its expansion to a college curriculum several years later.

Hill and Stone took their message to business groups, school campuses, and lecture halls all over the country, but they also took it to the nooks and crannies of society far beyond the limelight of television and radio coverage, where hope and achievement were distant concepts. They conducted classes in the poorest ghettos of America's sprawling cities. And they traveled to penitentiaries, where they conducted classes and circulated copies of *PMA Science of Success* home-study textbooks. They eventually promoted the program to prison systems throughout the country, citing results of an independent study that found inmates who became involved in self-improvement programs during their incarceration were far less likely to return to prison again.

On October 23, 1955, Napoleon Hill celebrated his seventy-first birthday. Only his immediate family and a few very close associates knew his actual age—in newspaper interviews and promotional literature he usually gave his age as 62 . . . or less. Even then, the most typical response from friends and new acquaintances alike was that Hill looked and acted like an even younger man.

This wasn't idle flattery. Photographs from the period depict a trim, dapper Napoleon Hill. The rigid, military bearing of his youth had matured into a more relaxed, aristocratic posture. His spectacles and gently receding hairline gave him a professorial aura. But his most striking feature, his eyes, still took in the world around him with vigor and animation.

Beyond his appearance, Hill's pace of daily activity was beyond the scope of imagination for a seventy-one year old. He logged tens of thousands of miles of travel each year, made dozens of speeches and lectures, wrote tens of thousands of words of manuscripts, speeches, promotional text, and radio and television scripts—all in addition to an unending progression of business lunches and dinners, consultations and conferences, meetings and phone calls.

Typical of the frenetic pace of Hill's life, he spent the Christmas of 1956 on the East Coast because of business commitments. Rather than spend the holiday alone in some hotel, he traveled to Gaffney, South Carolina, where Annie

Lou's sister, Leila, and nephew, Charles, were then living. It was the next best thing to being with Annie Lou, for the family bonds that had been forged between Napoleon and Leila and Charles during his courtship of Annie Lou had never weakened.

During his stay, Leila suggested that he and Annie Lou move to South Carolina so that Annie Lou would have family nearby during Nap's travels and to nurture family closeness year-round. Napoleon loved the idea, and shortly thereafter he and Annie Lou moved to Greenville, South Carolina. They once again had "family" and his commutes to Chicago became much shorter.

With that move, Napoleon Hill's life reached the pinnacle of satisfaction. He was still in love with Annie Lou, and she with him. He had family and friends. He had in W. Clement Stone a powerful patron, kindred spirit, and devoted friend all in one person. He was wealthy and secure. Napoleon Hill Associates had achieved financial viability. And his philosophy, his life's work, was reaching more millions of people with more impact than at any other time in his life.

Far from cutting back in his activities, he carved new goals and pursued them with unrelenting vigor. He and Stone embarked on long public-appearance tours in Puerto Rico in 1959, and in Australia and New Zealand in 1960. In between, there was a crowning achievement for both men: the release of *Success Through a Positive Mental Attitude,* coauthored by Stone and Hill.

The book was an instant hit and became a classic title in the self-help field with more than six hundred thousand copies sold in North America, Europe, and Asia. Stone did most of the writing, borrowing liberally from Hill's spoken and written thoughts. For once, Hill functioned as editor, consultant, and critic.

Success Through a Positive Mental Attitude bore a vague similarity to Hill's 1928 classic, *Law of Success*. Like that book, its theme was expressed in a stream of inspirational vignettes, anecdotes, and profiles of real people who had changed their lives by applying the principles of success. But *Success Through a Positive Mental Attitude* was a very modern version of *Law of Success*, and it bore the distinct motivational style of W. Clement Stone. Whereas the instructional homilies of the young Napoleon Hill were delivered with the rambling verve of a street-corner evangelist's sermon, Stone's message was tightly focused, his writing style was lean and fast-reading, and his parables dealt with unknowns as well as famous people.

While *Success Through a Positive Mental Attitude* was Stone's work, Hill's contributions were substantial. It was Hill who first suggested that Stone write the book, then convinced him that he was capable of writing a great book. This alone was a huge accomplishment. Despite all the time Stone put into the Science of Success and Napoleon Hill Associates, he was still immersed in running his huge company. To handle all his responsibilities, he was already working more than twelve hours a day, six days a week.

Inspired by his seventy-five-year-old workaholic friend and associate, Stone devised a simple, if superhuman, solution to the problem of finding time to write a book without cutting back on the time he needed to devote to his company. Since he only slept two or three hours a night anyway, Stone hired two more personal secretaries. He dictated his text to the secretaries, who worked in two shifts; when the last secretary left for the night, he continued working on a dictaphone. As the secretaries finished typing his dictation each day, transcripts of the material for *Success Through a Positive Mental Attitude* were passed to Hill for comments and criticism.

This killing pace appealed to both men. Over the next two years, Stone wrote *The Success System that Never Fails* on his own, and Hill published *Grow Rich With Peace of Mind* in 1967.

As Napoleon Hill celebrated his birthday on October 23, 1961, he was mulling one of the most unlikely birthday wishes a seventy-eight-year-old man ever contemplated. Flushed with the success of his ten-year association with Stone, Napoleon wanted to take on an awesome new challenge: He wanted to create a franchise business that would make his philosophy of success a staple in nearly every American's life.

The concept was simple enough. Just as he and Stone had trained people to teach Science of Success classes in the 1950s, they would now recruit entrepreneurs all over the world to purchase Napoleon Hill franchises. Each entrepreneur would be licensed and trained to promote and conduct local classes and home-study programs, as well as the many other products developed by Napoleon Hill Associates. Each franchise owner would then hire his or her own sales and administrative staff and penetrate every institution, organization, and neighborhood in their marketing area.

Hill had tried the basic concept several times in the distant past without success, but things were different now. He was far more famous and influential than ever before, and, even more important, he had W. Clement Stone's model to follow: His franchise concept was built along the same lines as Stone's incredibly successful sales organization.

Stone was astonished and intrigued that his aged friend would contemplate such a challenging project. It had taken a young, vigorous W. Clement Stone more than a decade of endless weeks and sleepless nights to get Combined Insurance Company of America's sales organization established. He could hardly believe that his wealthy, famous, established friend could want to start such an undertaking at the age of seventy-eight. Stone himself could not, he regretfully informed Hill. Thanks in part to Hill, Stone's insurance empire had swelled enormously in size and complexity; it was one of the largest privately owned companies in the United States, and it was still growing. There was no way he could invest the time required to establish a franchise business and continue running his company.

Despite Stone's counseling to the contrary, Napoleon could not resist trying to create one more grandiose chapter in his life's work. Both men lived by the credo, "What the mind of man can conceive, it can achieve," and both men understood that franchising was a concept that had three-dimensional reality in Hill's mind at that point. Marveling at his septuagenarian friend's ambition, Stone signed over virtually all of the assets of Napoleon Hill Associates to Hill and stepped aside. The two men ended their business partnership the same way it began—with a handshake—but their friendship would continue unabated for years to come.

CHAPTER 9

1962-1994

America's pulse was pounding with the idealism of John F. Kennedy's New Frontier program as Napoleon and Annie Lou Hill signed the articles of incorporation for their new Napoleon Hill Foundation in August 1962. It was a time when Americans set their sights high, with thoughts of reaching the moon, eradicating inequality and poverty, and dedicating themselves to their country.

Although Napoleon Hill detested the government-subsidized social programs of JFK's "Camelot"—he saw them as a narcotic that would rob the underprivileged of both the will and the means to succeed—few Americans were more dedicated to the principles of public service, equality, and reaching for unthinkable heights. Indeed, from the day he wrote the concept for *Hill's Golden Rule* magazine in 1918, his entire career had been devoted to those very ideas.

It was the dawn of the golden age of high-minded, pub-lic-welfare, activist organizations. Established groups would see their memberships and influence grow exponentially, and hundreds of new groups were formed. Over the next quarter century they would, collectively, seek to protect human rights, defend the indigent, educate the mentally handicapped, purify the air and water, preserve the land, end warfare, and pursue hundreds of other noble causes.

Like most of these organizations, the Napoleon Hill Foundation grew from idealistic roots. Unlike most, however, the Foundation's roots traced back to a seed planted more than a half century before, when a starstruck Appalachian youth was given a lifelong mission by the wealthiest man in America. And the Foundation also differed from most other groups in its focus: Rather than seeking to influence government policy or public opinion, it was dedicated to nurturing *personal* achievement and inspiring individuals to use their own devices to overcome barriers to success.

The Foundation's articles of incorporation specified that it was "not organized for the purpose of profit or gain to the members." The corporation's purpose was listed as, "to teach . . . and to perpetuate the lifetime research, writings and teachings of . . . Dr. Napoleon Hill, as sponsored by Andrew Carnegie." The Foundation consisted of three officers and trustees—Napoleon, Annie Lou, and Hill's attorney.

From a small office in Columbia, South Carolina, the trustees began building the Foundation's programs. Their agenda focused on rehabilitation programs for prison inmates, an international leadership school, and a national franchising program that would train and license individual entrepreneurs to market courses and literature for profit.

In truth, though, the development of the Foundation as an effective, directed organization progressed slowly. Hill, still in great demand as a speaker, kept up a frenetic pace of lectures and personal appearances all over the country. It was an awesome display of energy and commitment by a man nearly eighty years old.

Napoleon's speaking engagements during this period ran the familiar gamut of business and community groups, prisons, and high schools and colleges. One especially interesting appearance came in 1962 at a Kansas City, Kansas, high school with a predominantly black student body. Dr. Martin Luther King's passive resistance campaign for equal rights was nearing its zenith, and millions of African-Americans were beginning to resist the notion that their prospects in life were limited by their race. Napoleon was introduced by the man who arranged his appearance—James Browne, a successful black entrepreneur who was then the president of the Crusader Life Insurance Company. Browne was also a student of Hill's.

Napoleon's speech rated page-one, lead-story coverage in the school's newspaper. The article described a vintage Hill lecture—equal measures of philosophy and anecdote, spiced with a dash of overstatement, and blended into an improvisational hour or so of inspiration. The overstatement, as always, concerned Hill's early achievements—he described himself as a millionaire at age twenty-one. It was a forgivable legacy of years of struggling for attention and acceptance. Ironically, the fact that his millionaire status was achieved only after seventy years of perseverance would have been even more inspirational and instructive for any audience in 1962.

Still, Hill's message came through loud and clear. A young student-journalist recorded this report for Sumner High School's newspaper, *The Courier:*

> "Men are born," he said, "with two envelopes in their hands. In one envelope are the penalties for not realizing and embracing the abilities of the mind. In the other are the rewards for realizing and embracing the mind's abilities."

Factors for Success

He believes that there are four factors without which no man can rise above mediocrity:

- Purpose. One should know where he is going and how he is going to get there.

- Going the extra mile. There is no success in doing no more than what is expected or just doing enough to keep up with "Joe."

- Mastermind Theory. Cooperation with two or more people who are already successful in order to bring about a definite harmony will give one models and goals to shoot for.

- Applied Faith. Just believing in God is not enough. This belief must be made a part of man's everyday life.

Mr. Hill, jokingly called "Nap the Sap" because he accepted the job of advisor to President Roosevelt for one dollar a year, believes so strongly in these four factors that he has established schools in Australia and New Zealand. Students in these schools are taught the importance of positive thinking. They are also taught the value of passive resistance.

Convert Defeat

On the matter of passive resistance, Mr. Hill said, "I have never accepted anything from life that I didn't want. Every failure and defeat should be converted into something constructive.

. . . At the conclusion of his speech Mr. Hill gave an original prayer which he uses at the beginning and end of each day:

"O, Infinite Intelligence, I ask not for more blessings but for more wisdom with which to enjoy the blessings with which you endowed me at birth consisting of my sole right to take possession of my own mind and direct it to ends of my own choice. Amen."

★ ★ ★

Early in 1964, several significant changes came to the Napoleon Hill Foundation. At its board of trustees meeting in January, Hill's attorney resigned from the board and purchased rights to the Napoleon Hill Academy from the Foundation. The Academy was the fledgling program designed to establish franchised local businesses to teach the principles of success and distribute the Foundation's literature and books. The franchising concept was inspired by W. Clement Stone's fabulously successful sales organization: In Stone's sales force, each salesperson was an independent businessperson. He or she bought policies from Stone's company at a wholesale price, then sold them at retail and kept the profits.

Stone's franchise-type approach to selling insurance made Combined Insurance a partnership of thousands of small businesses, rather than a behemoth company with thousands of employees. There were no income restrictions on any partner, no jealousies about promotions: Those who wanted to get richer simply worked harder and smarter.

Hill's dream was to apply the same concept to marketing his philosophy of success. Locally owned, independent Napoleon Hill Academy franchises would buy educational materials, books, films, and records from the Foundation and conduct their own for-profit classes, seminars, and similar services. Hill reasoned that the profit motive would sustain hundreds, perhaps thousands, of people to promote and teach the principles of success to millions and provide a steady stream of income to support the Foundation.

As W. Clement Stone had warned, however, the creation of a successful franchise program required great amounts of time, organization and single-minded dedication—and Napoleon had finally come to realize that, at eighty years of age, he was not willing to forego all his other pursuits for this one dream. He and the attorney agreed that the Academy's best chance for success was to make it the sole enterprise of one capable man.

When the sale of the Academy was consummated, Napoleon and Annie Lou decided to expand the board of trustees to five people and get the Foundation moving ahead in earnest. They did. By March 1964, the Foundation had a five-member board, and was ready to procure its own executive offices.

The bylaws formally stated the Foundation's goals, which were to communicate the philosophy of success to people around the world. The board members voted unanimously to focus especially on prisons, boys clubs, and mental health institutions, and they discussed ways to maximize the visibility of the Foundation and its programs in conjunction with Napoleon's personal appearances on radio and television, and before live crowds.

Napoleon Hill turned eighty-one years old in October 1964. He still traveled, though not as much. And he still drove his own automobile.

It was at about this time in his life that Napoleon and Annie Lou drove one day from their home near Greenville to visit Annie Lou's sister, Leila. Leila had married Ben Hatcher and moved to Gaffney, South Carolina. The close-knit ties between Leila, Annie Lou, and Napoleon had, if anything, become stronger during that time: Just as Napoleon had been taken into the circle in the 1940s, Ben and his in-laws Napoleon and Annie Lou had long since become great friends and supportive family.

Napoleon and Annie Lou's visit had the makings of a somber occasion. They had discussed the fact that with Napoleon entering his eighties and Annie Lou nearing seventy years of age, death was something for which they needed to be prepared. They came to Gaffney on this day to buy plots in Ben Hatcher's cemetery. They had no relatives in

Greenville, and they wanted to be sure their graves would have proper care after they were gone, they explained to Leila and Ben. They also wanted their graves to be adjacent to those of Leila and Ben.

"So we all went up to the Frederick Memorial Gardens," recalled Leila. "Napoleon said, 'Ben, I want these plots to be close to the entrance to the Gardens, for I want to be sure I get on that first chariot load—but before it comes, you and I can get up at night and go fishing in the lake and Annie Lou and Leila can get up and swap recipes.' "

Although Napoleon was prepared for death, he was nowhere near done living. The minutes of the 1965 board meetings of the Foundation showed that he had pursued his prison rehabilitation plan with full vigor; a program of classes for inmates of South Carolina penal institutions was ready for launch. In addition, the Foundation had received glowing publicity in *Success World* magazine to complement exposures linked to Hill's appearances and interviews. A year later, the Internal Revenue Service confirmed the Foundation's tax-exempt status, fulfilling another of Hill's primary objectives for the organization.

But this was also a time when Napoleon began slowing down, both in his personal appearances and in his Foundation activities. After eight decades of toil, turmoil, and evangelism, he wanted to spend more time with Annie Lou. He was finally ready to enjoy a more leisurely pace of life. Indeed, leisure was, perhaps, the only life experience he had not sampled in his long and fruitful career.

Napoleon never fully retired from the Foundation, but he delegated more and more of his authority and responsibility to the organization's board members and employees. Similarly, until his health began to fail in the late sixties, Hill delighted in making an occasional speech or public appearance.

Much of Hill's work in the mid-sixties seemed oriented toward tying up the loose ends of his life's work—establishing a line of succession so that others would communicate the philosophy of success when he was gone, and recognizing the contributions of those who had championed his cause over the years. The most poignant moment in this, his last campaign, came in 1964 when Hill traveled to Chicago to pay tribute to W. Clement Stone. Standing before a small gathering of Stone's top managers and salespeople, Hill presented Stone with a framed declaration, which read, in part:

"Let it be known that the honorable W. Clement Stone has been selected by Dr. Napoleon Hill, author of *The Science of Personal Achievement,* as the third most outstanding individual to utilize the 17 principles of *The Science of Personal Achievement.* First place recognition has been given to Andrew Carnegie; second place to Thomas Alva Edison; and third place to the aforementioned individual who with great skill, patience, persistency, and courage has become a living testimony to the truth that whatever the mind of man can conceive and believe, it can also achieve."

Thoroughly moved by Hill's gesture, Stone accepted the document and spoke of the impact Napoleon and his philosophy had had on Stone's own life and the lives of thousands of others. "Twelve years ago this month," Stone recalled, "Napoleon Hill and I met for the first time, and I was so enthused that I suggested he come out of retirement . . . and devote the rest of his life to completing his life's work. . . . He agreed on one condition: that I be his general manager. . . . I accepted.

"Now something wonderful happened, something that completely changed the course of my life, and, I believe, the lives of many others. For in our effort to help Napoleon Hill and the work to which he was dedicated, I began to engage in public speaking. . . . I began writing editorials and sales articles . . . and it was because of him that I began to write books."

When Stone was done, he turned the podium over to Napoleon Hill. Speaking without notes in his customary ramrod-straight posture, relying on vocal inflection to seize and hold his audience's attention, Napoleon delivered a series of funny stories and anecdotes, then took his audience back more than a half century to the very origins of his philosophy of success:

> When I went to see Mr. Andrew Carnegie in 1908, I went there to write a story about him. He gave me three hours and when the three hours were up, he said, "Now this interview is just beginning. Come down to the house and stay all night and we can take it up after dinner."
>
> I was glad he said come on down to the house. If he had said go over to the hotel . . . and come back tomorrow I would have been sunk because I had just about enough money in my pocket to pay my way back to Washington, D.C.
>
> After dinner he started in and he said, "now what this world needs is a new philosophy based upon the know-how of men like myself who have learned by the trial and error method what will succeed and what will not." He told me how long it would take to organize the philosophy, whose help one would have to have, what it would do for unborn generations, and certainly what it would do for the men who organized it.
>
> He built up one of the most beautiful pictures I ever saw and I wondered . . . why was he doing that? Well, I found out at the end of the third day. He said, "Now, I've been talking to you for three days about this new philosophy, about the need for it, about where the information can be had to organize it. I wish to ask you a question and

don't answer that question until you make up your mind whether it's yes or no.

"If I commission you to become the author of this philosophy, give you a letter of introduction to men whose help you have to have, are you willing to devote 20 years to research? Because that is just about how long it would take, earning your own way as you go along, without any subsidy from me except traveling expenses. Yes or no?"

What would you have said? What would you have done if you had been sitting there with practically no money— in front of the richest man in the world, who wanted you to go to work for 20 years without any compensation. What would you have said?

Well, that's exactly what I tried to say. What's in your mind right now.

I can think of a dozen reasons, yes, 20 of them, why I couldn't possibly do that. In the first place, I didn't have enough education to be with the men whose collaboration I would have to have, successful men like Mr. Carnegie. I only made high school by the skin of my teeth—and if I hadn't had much better teeth than I have now I wouldn't have made it.

Now, you don't know what I'm talking about. You're young!

And in the second place, I didn't have enough money to carry me for 20 years. And in the third place, and this was more serious than the other two, I wasn't absolutely sure about the meaning of the word *philosophy,* which Mr. Carnegie had been kicking around for three days and nights.

But finally, something inside of me said, "Tell him you'll do it" and I blurted it out. I said, "Mr. Carnegie, I not only accept the commission you have offered me, but you may depend upon it, sir, that I will complete the job" and he grabbed me by the hand and shook my hand and said "I not only like what you did, but I like the way you did it, and you've got the job!" And I thought, "My God, what have I got?"

Before I left, and this is the reason I'm telling you this story, he said "20 years is a long time, the conditions I have imposed upon you are very stringent, the temptations for you to quit and get into something else will be many, so I'm going to give you a formula that will enable you to bridge these temptations when they come and keep on keeping on." I was taking this all down in shorthand. He said "I want you to write very slowly and take down this formula. Here it comes:

"Andrew Carnegie, I'm not only going to equal your achievements in life, but I'm going to challenge you at the post and pass you at the grandstand." And I threw my pencil down. I said "Mr. Carnegie, you know very well I'm not going to be able to do that." He said "Of course I know you're not going to be able to do that unless or until you believe it. But if you believe it, you will."

Now he said, "will you try it out for 30 days—just try it for 30 days" and I said, "Oh yes, I can do that with my fingers crossed on both hands." I knew very well it was a foolish thing for me to try, but I promised him that I would.

I went back to Washington [where] my brother and I . . . had an apartment. I didn't want my brother to know what a fool I had made of myself, so when I started to repeat this formula, I went in the bathroom and closed the door real tight and got up real close to the glass. I almost whispered it. And as I turned around I saw in my mind's eye the real Napoleon Hill standing there and I said: "You damn liar! You know very well you're not going to be [I'm quoting what Napoleon Hill says then] able to do that." And that went on for almost a week and I felt like somebody who is cheating himself. I said that it was a foolish thing and I almost backed out on Mr. Carnegie. I thought maybe he's lost his mind . . . it was too absurd for words.

Then about the end of the first week, something inside of me said, look here, Andrew Carnegie has the reputation of being the best judge and the best picker of men in the world. And he's also the richest man in the world, and maybe he's found something in you that you didn't know was there. Why don't you change your mental attitude and start expecting to find something good out of it?

Ladies and gentlemen, I changed my mental attitude and I want to tell you that by the end of the month, I not only believed that I was going to catch up with Mr. Carnegie and excel him, but I knew down deep in my heart with all of my heart . . . that I would do it.

And may I very modestly tell you that long since have I far outdistanced and passed Andrew Carnegie. I don't have as many millions of dollars as he had, but I have all that I need. And I've made more millionaires than Mr. Carnegie ever made. I don't think he ever made 20 at most, maybe not that many. And where he has been of help to only hundreds of people, I have been of help to millions of people throughout the free world.

. . . And that is the greatest of my riches. I've helped people to find themselves, to find their own minds, to discover better ways of relating themselves to other people. I don't know how long I'm going to live yet—I'm 81 years young and I have laid out another 25-year program—but I do tell you one thing: as long as I live, I'm going to keep on keeping on going out of my way to render useful service for other people wherever I find the opportunity to do it. And I hope with all my heart and soul that some one word I have spoken here today will give you an introspective view of your own mind, a better understanding of it, a determination that from here on out you're not only going to sell the other people you come in contact with, but above all, you're going to sell the man who walks around under your hat and sell him good. I thank you.

As he neared the age of eighty-four, Napoleon Hill's health finally began to fail. Plagued by cataracts, he was forced to stop driving and had to use a huge magnifying glass to read. In 1968 he underwent cataract surgery.

A year later, in April 1969, Senator Jennings Randolph dashed off a note to W. Clement Stone, informing him of the fact that Napoleon was once again in the hospital. Sensing that the end was near for Napoleon, Randolph added, "We have both been blessed by his service to mankind."

Napoleon had, indeed, been stricken with a debilitating cerebral hemorrhage. His physicians held out little hope of survival. However, Hill had never been one to give in easily and resisted fatality. Though he would never recover the full vitality that had marked his long life, he lived to celebrate two more birthdays with his beloved Annie Lou and Leila. He died on November 8, 1970, at the age of eighty-seven.

Napoleon Hill's eulogy was delivered by Lee Braxton, a Tulsa, Oklahoma, businessman who had been a longtime supporter and personal friend of Hill's. He spoke of the man and his work interchangeably, like Hill himself had. "One of his great discoveries," said Braxton, "is the free use of our minds, believing that whatever the mind of man can conceive and believe, it can achieve."

Braxton ended on a similar note: "The mortal remains will soon go back to earth, to God who gave it, but Dr. Napoleon Hill will live on in the minds and hearts of millions as long as men are free to think and act."

EPILOGUE

Napoleon Hill's greatest desires at the time of his death were that Annie Lou be financially secure, and that his life's work be perpetuated by the Napoleon Hill Foundation.

Since he left Annie Lou a millionaire, her comfort was assured.

Annie Lou Hill was nearly eighty-eight years old as she surveyed the Napoleon Hill Foundation and tried to contemplate its future. She arrived at a course of action quickly and acted decisively, creating a new board of trustees that would plan and guide the foundation.

Annie Lou had never been one for half measures. The people she convinced to lead the foundation were individuals of great accomplishment, who were longtime advocates for Napoleon Hill principles. Two were giant public figures: W. Clement Stone, who agreed to take the helm, and United States Senator Jennings Randolph of West Virginia, who had supported Hill and his work for decades.

Three other board members were not public figures but would play extraordinary roles in directing the foundation's growth into the nineties.

One was Dr. Charles Johnson, M.D., Leila's son and Annie Lou's beloved nephew. Johnson's relationship with Napoleon Hill was unique and touching. It had begun in 1941, when Johnson was four years old and Napoleon married Annie Lou and moved into the Clinton, South Carolina, apartment building where he and his mother and Annie Lou lived. The two became great pals, each finding in the other something missing in his life—for Johnson, a father figure; for Napoleon, as fatherly uncle, a chance to savor some portion of the delights of parenthood that he had denied himself as a young, career-obsessed father. The attachment between Charles and Napoleon stayed strong through the years. Indeed, when Charles became dissatisfied with his college major, it was Napoleon who encouraged him to pursue his dream of becoming a doctor, and it was Napoleon who helped finance the extraordinary costs of medical school.

Another was Michael J. Ritt, Jr., a Combined Insurance Company vice-president who had worked closely with Hill and Stone in the Napoleon Hill Associates era. His writing and promotional talents had been instrumental in creating public awareness of the organization's courses, lectures, and other activities. Most of all, perhaps, it was Ritt who had analyzed the early Napoleon Hill Associates ventures and recommended and redesigned specific new programs that had the best potential for making the foundation financially self-sufficient.

Even before convening the new board, Stone solicited expert consultation on how to manage a successful foundation. He got the advice he needed by turning to Senator Strom Thurmond, who gave him full access to Dr. Horace Fleming, the man who directed the Strom Thurmond Institute. Fleming also became a member of the Napoleon Hill Foundation's new board of directors.

Thus prepared, Stone covered a lot of ground in the first board meeting. With the approval of the other board mem-

bers and Annie Lou Hill, he asked Michael Ritt to become
the foundation's executive director and secretary-treasurer.
Ritt accepted. Then he laid out a financial plan for the
foundation, which at that point had no capital and no revenue-generating programs in place. Stone offered to cover
all foundation expenses for first-year salaries, office space,
promotional efforts, and everything else required to jump-
start the organization. After the first year he continued to
lend the foundation whatever capital it needed, interest free.
But, he stressed, the foundation must develop a program to
make it financially self-sufficient as soon as possible. Since
achieving financial self-sufficiency in 1987, the Napoleon
Hill Foundation has continued to expand its programs and
economic base.

The Napoleon Hill Foundation continues its namesake's
legacy today. It remains a non-profit charitable institution
whose mission is "To Make the World a Better Place in
Which to Live" by teaching the principles of leadership, self-
motivation, and individual achievement throughout the
world in the various media formats.

> The foundation's goals are to disseminate the Napoleon
> Hill philosophy of personal achievement to colleges, uni-
> versities, school systems, business and industry, and the
> prison system.
>
> To share Napoleon Hill's philosophy of personal
> achievement—helping individuals reach their highest lev-
> els of personal accomplishment and self-fulfillment.
>
> To teach the principles of success and self-motivation to
> men and women by helping them discover the power
> within themselves so they may acquire the "True Riches
> of Life" and reach their own self-fulfillment.

The reemergence of the foundation, its growth, and its
determination to pursue an ever larger agenda marked a

changing of the guard of Napoleon Hill's philosophy of personal achievement. It began in the early years of the twentieth century, as a grand idea in the mind of Andrew Carnegie. It became the grand obsession of Hill. Now his works live on more than ninety years after Carnegie started the saga, more than a half century after *Think and Grow Rich!* became the greatest self-help best-seller of its time. And as the Napoleon Hill Foundation flourishes, so does Napoleon Hill's final dream: to help this and future generations achieve all they want from life without violating the laws of God and the rights of their fellow man.

INDEX

Upon request, the owner of this book may receive an autographed bookplate bearing the signature of Napoleon Hill. Address your request to the Napoleon Hill Foundation, 1440 Paddock Drive, Northbrook, Illinois 60062, enclosing a large, self-addressed, stamped envelope. With this bookplate you will receive a copy of one of Dr. Hill's famous success essays.

· A NOTE ON THE TYPE ·

The typeface used in this book is a version of Bembo, issued by
Monotype in 1929 and based on the first "old style" roman typeface,
which was designed for the publication, by the great Venetian
printer Aldus Manutius (1450–1515), of Pietro Bembo's De Ætna
(1495). Among the first to use octavo format, making his books
cheaper and more portable, Aldus might have grown rich printing
as he did a thousand volumes per month—an extraordinary number
for the time—had his books not been mercilessly pirated. The
counterfeits did, however, spread the new typefaces throughout
Europe, and they were widely imitated. The so-called Aldine romans
were actually designed by the man who cut the type for Aldus,
Francesco Griffo (d. 1519). Griffo fought with Manutius over credit
for the designs and was later hanged after killing his brother-in-law
with an iron bar.